□□□Rethinking the Constitution

An Anthology of Japanese Opinion

□□□Rethinking the Constitution

An Anthology of Japanese Opinion

The Constitution of Japan Project 2004

Translated by Fred Uleman

Published by **Japan Research Inc.**

ISBN 1-4196-4165-4

originally published by Kodansha under the title
Nihon no Kenpou: Kokumin Shuken no Ronten
© The Constitution of Japan Project 2004

Translation © Fred Uleman 2006
Published by Japan Research Inc.
Shinmaruko-cho 749-6-104, Nakahara-ku, Kawasaki 211-0005, Japan
Phone: +81 3 3400 2130
Fax: +81 3 3406 7730
Email: fuleman@jpnres.com

□□□ Contents

□□□ Translator's Preface

THERE IS INCREASING talk of amending the Japanese Constitution, but proponents of amending the Constitution have long been very visible – as have been opponents. Both sides have been here ever since the Constitution was adopted in 1946. Yet the over-my-dead-body opponents – those who fear Article 9's anti-war stance will be gutted – have lost considerable ground over the last decade or so, which in turn has moved the issue to the political forefront.

This is not an issue that will be decided easily or even finally. Even after a decision is made to amend – or not amend – the Constitution, there are likely to be further calls for revision. It is one of Japanese politics' perennial issues. It is a core issue. And to paraphrase, it is too important to be left to the politicians.

When I saw Kodansha's *Nihon no Kenpou: Kokumin Shuken no Ronten* in the bookstore, I bought it for its wide range of authors – many of them not the usual suspects. After I read it, I thought, "Somebody should translate this." But Kodansha said they had no plans for an English edition. So I took it upon myself. Happily, many friends helped, and I am immensely grateful to them. This includes not only Lynette Perkins, who did the initial translations of a number of essays, but many other people as well. Especially important were Igari Noriko, who graciously reviewed all of the translations to make sure the English accurately reflects the full sense of the Japanese; Susan Schmidt, who went over the entire book from an English editor's perspective, making many valuable suggestions in the process; and Chris Ryal, who undertook the design and production. This has been a labor of love for all concerned – a work undertaken because we believe it essential that anyone commenting on the Japanese Constitution's future be aware of what "Japanese opinion" thinks.

This is a sampler as of mid- 2004. Some of the essays may have been overtaken by subsequent events, but none has been mooted. All are just as relevant now as they were when this book first came out in Japanese. I hope you find them interesting reading.

Some technical notes

Names are given in the standard order of the individual's language. For Japanese, this means family name first.

Unless otherwise indicated, the translations of book and other titles are for information only.

With the exception of proper nouns that already have firmly established romanizations (e.g., Tokyo and Osaka), Japanese has been romanized so that inputting it on your computer can call up the correct kanji. Thus Katou (and not Katoh) to indicate that the "o" is an extended vowel. This is instead of using macrons. That said, there is one exception: Kawamoto Yuko – who explicitly requested that her given name be written "Yuko" instead of "Yuuko" even though the "u" is an extended vowel in Japanese.

Some of the essays were based upon interviews with the authors, the authors then having final approval of the text ghosted by the editorial team. These interview-based essays have been so marked.

□□□Introduction

POLITICIANS, ACADEMICS, AND the mass media are devoting considerable attention to the question of possibly amending the Constitution, and this issue is looming ever larger. Yet even though sovereignty theoretically rests with the people, the discussion seems to be paying little or no attention to "the people." That is wrong. The Constitution is not something that a small cabal of people can amend at will. Nor should it be amended simply to make it easier for the ruling class to wield state power. Now is the time for all of the people to speak up and to assert their rights. That is why this book has been compiled and published – to facilitate greater popular involvement in this critical debate.

Our modern democracy's Constitution is a far cry from the simple 17-article moral code that Prince Shotoku proclaimed in 604. There are some who argue that Japanese society is dysfunctional because the current Constitution does not dwell on moral edicts – people who would bring back the old moralistic injunctions – but such talk has no place in any serious discussion of amending the Constitution of a modern democracy. Rather, such comments are simply the grumblings of people who were educated during the war and, having never adapted to democracy, mutter, "Young people these days are no good. Bring back the draft. Bring back the ancient ethical moralism."

That is not what the Constitution is for. Rather, the Constitution is an essential breakwater – a crucial defense protecting the people against the excesses of state authority. As such, it is a basic legal document curtailing and limiting the government so as to ensure that the people are fully able to enjoy their fundamental human rights.

This bears repeating. The Constitution is not to benefit state authority. The Constitution is to benefit the people. Realizing that, this book begins with the preambles from a number of Constitutions from around the world. As seen in these examples, the only Constitutions that aggrandize the state are those from the socialist states. The "global standard" is for the Constitution to be a defense of the people's rights.

Following the new Constitution's promulgation in 1946, the Ministry of Education issued a side-reader for first-year junior high school students entitled *Atarashii Kenpou no Hanashi* (The Story of the New Constitution), which included the following section on popular sovereignty: "You are all Japanese citizens. You are all the citizens in whom sovereignty resides. Yet sovereignty rests with the Japanese citizenry as a whole. It is not something that is divided up and held by each individual. Much less does it mean that each of you has special privileges and can do entirely as you please." Even here, the state seems to be doing its best to hem in individual initiative. What is wrong with people doing as they please? What is wrong with people believing they are privileged?

At the International Tribunal for the Far East, Japanese military officers who were asked why they had waged the war typically answered: "Personally, I thought it was a bad idea, but I had my orders." Sadly, this mentality seems to persist even today, nearly 60 years later. Why can't we break free of this?

This volume is a collection of hints intended to help you, the reader, think about the Constitution as a personal document. It is common today to see young people taking part in volunteer activities. This is quite natural and very welcome. Individual initiative benefits the whole community. Yet older generations did not have the same volunteer spirit. Rather, the early postwar years were marked by a clear delineation between the public sector (government) and the private sector (the governed), and people forgot that "the public" is actually a collective form of "the individual." The fact that few older people have this understanding of "public" has created problems for Japan. For example, they tend to think of the Constitution – that most public of documents – as somebody else's jurisdiction. They tend to think a national referendum is something that happens somewhere else.

As a result, Japanese society has come to resemble a small town in which a few officials run everything to benefit their friends and associates. Even professional baseball, which is ostensibly a public-interest business, has recently evidenced this crony capitalism in the owners' efforts to change the rules for their own benefit. Even though this old cronyism no longer works, there are some people who cling stubbornly to its vestiges. (In professional baseball, this is illustrated by the way everything seems to revolve around the Yomiuri Giants.) These people have forgotten the most important stakeholders. They have forgotten that the most important people are not the front offices, not the media, and not even the players – much less the owners. The most important people are the fans who love the game. As such, the recent dust-up in professional baseball bears a striking resemblance to the debate over the Constitution. Both reek of a leave-it-to-the-powers-that-be (which does not just mean the government) attitude and a complacency induced by feelings of helplessness. "Let's not get involved. Things'll work out somehow." This is still the dominant mindset in all too many areas, and it marks a depressing abdication of the public.

This abdication of the public, this village cronyism, and this deference to officialdom are engendered and reinforced by the drumbeat of exhortations that "When you think about yourself, you should also think about the rest of your community" and "There is no individual except within the context of the group." To get away from this, it is important to realize that the individual is the self – and the community comes into being only when each individual is considerate and thoughtful toward other individuals. In thinking about the Constitution in this time of transition, it is essential we realize that it is the individual – the self – that interacts as a sovereign entity with the state. The state will not change unless each individual exercises sovereign initiative. The very concept of popular sovereignty means that each and every individual has the sovereign authority to decide what kind of a state and what kind of a Constitution he or she wants for the future.

There is today considerable momentum for changing social structures. And there are some politicians who pompously proclaim this "the greatest transformation since the Meiji Restoration" (of 1868). But we do not need this grandstanding. If the 1990s have taught us anything at all, they have taught that eloquent speeches and empty posturing do not make for meaningful reforms. At the same time, they have shown that Japan has no future unless the people get over their somebody-else'll-do-it mindset and start thinking in I'll-do-it terms.

The first step is to read the Constitution – not as a plaything for politicians but as a crucial document protecting and preserving our fundamental rights. And then read the many opinions expressed in this book – weighing each of them against the standard of popular sovereignty. What kind of a Constitution will allow you to live the kind of life you want to live? This is the perspective to take when thinking about the Constitution. For underlying everything has to be the fundamental principle of popular sovereignty. Perhaps the Constitution should be amended. Perhaps not. It is up to you – the people. It is for you to decide.

– The Constitution of Japan Project 2004 Team

■□□ About the Constitution

A Constitution is ...

A Constitution is an expression of a nation's ideals and how it sees itself. This is especially true of the Preamble, and Preambles are devoted to elucidating what the country stands for. As such, it is often possible to get a good idea of the country's basic stance just by looking at the Preamble to its Constitution. It is thus instructive to look here at Preambles from a range of countries, from the United States to North Korea. What do they say? What do they tell us?

■□□ Preambles from Around the World

Japan (1946)

WE, THE JAPANESE people, acting through our duly elected representatives in the National Diet, determined that we shall secure for ourselves and our posterity the fruits of peaceful cooperation with all nations and the blessings of liberty throughout this land, and resolved that never again shall we be visited with the horrors of war through the action of government, do proclaim that sovereign power resides with the people and do firmly establish this Constitution. Government is a sacred trust of the people, the authority for which is derived from the people, the powers of which are exercised by the representatives of the people, and the benefits of which are enjoyed by the people. This is a universal principle of mankind upon which this Constitution is founded. We reject and revoke all constitutions, laws, ordinances, and rescripts in conflict herewith.

We, the Japanese people, desire peace for all time and are deeply conscious of the high ideals controlling human relationship, and we have determined to preserve our security and existence, trusting in the justice and faith of the peace-loving peoples of the world. We desire to occupy an honored place in an international society striving for the preservation of peace, and the banishment of tyranny and slavery, oppression and intolerance for all time from the earth. We recognize that all peoples of the world have the right to live in peace, free from fear and want.

We believe that no nation is responsible to itself alone, but that laws of political morality are universal; and that obedience to such laws is incumbent upon all nations who would sustain their own sovereignty and justify their sovereign relationship with other nations.

We, the Japanese people, pledge our national honor to accomplish these high ideals and purposes with all our resources.

United States of America (1788)

WE THE PEOPLE of the United States, in order to form a more perfect Union, establish justice, insure domestic tranquility, provide for the common defence, promote the general welfare, and secure the blessings of liberty to ourselves and our posterity, do ordain and establish this Constitution for the United States of America.

France (Fifth Republic) (1958)

THE FRENCH PEOPLE hereby solemnly proclaim their dedication to the Rights of Man and the principle of national sovereignty as defined by the Declaration of 1789, reaffirmed and complemented by the Preamble to the 1946 Constitution.

By virtue of these principles and that of the free determination of peoples, the Republic offers to the Overseas Territories expressly desiring this to adhere to them new institutions based on the common ideal of liberty, equality, and fraternity and conceived with a view to their democratic evolution.

Germany (1949)

CONSCIOUS OF THEIR responsibility before God and men, animated by the purpose to serve world peace as an equal partner in a unified Europe, the German People have adopted, by virtue of their constituent power, this Constitution. The Germans in the States of Baden-Wurttemberg, Bavaria, Berlin, Brandenburg, Bremen, Hamburg, Hesse, Lower Saxony, Mecklenburg-Western Pomerania, North Rhine-Westphalia, Rhineland-Palatinate, Saarland, Saxony, Saxony-Anhalt, Schleswig-Holstein and Thuringia have achieved the unity and freedom of Germany in free self-determination. This Constitution is thus valid for the entire German People.

(*The German Constitution was written and adopted in 1945. The Preamble was amended with unification in 1990.*)

Spain (1978)

THE SPANISH NATION, desiring to establish justice, liberty and security and to promote the good of its members, in the exercise of its sovereignty, proclaims its will to:

guarantee democratic co-existence under the Constitution and the law, consistent with a just social and economic order;

consolidate a State of Law which assures the rule of law as an expression of the popular will;

protect all Spaniards and peoples of Spain in the exercise of human rights, of their cultures and traditions, and of their languages and institutions

promote the progress of culture and of the economy in order to ensure a worthy quality of life for all;

establish a democratic and advanced society, and

collaborate in the strengthening of peaceful relations and effective co-operation amongst all the peoples of the World

Wherefore, the Cortes pass and the Spanish people ratify the following.

Russian Federation (1993)

WE, THE MULTINATIONAL people of the Russian Federation, united by a common destiny on our land, asserting human rights and liberties, civil peace and accord, preserving the historic unity of the state, proceeding from the commonly recognized principles of equality and self-determination of the peoples honoring the memory of our ancestors, who have passed on to us love of and respect for our homeland and faith in good and justice, reviving the sovereign statehood of Russia and asserting its immutable democratic foundations, striving to secure the wellbeing and prosperity of Russia and proceeding from a sense of responsibility for our homeland before the present and future generations, and being aware of ourselves as part of the world community, hereby approve the Constitution of the Russian Federation.

Cuba (from Preamble and Article 1) (1992)

WE, CUBAN CITIZENS ... declare our will that the law of laws of the Republic be guided by the following strong desire of José Martí, at last achieved;

"I want the fundamental law of our republic to be the tribute of Cubans to the full dignity of man";

and adopt by means of our free vote in a referendum, the following:

Cuba is an independent and sovereign socialist state of workers, organized with all and for the good of all as a united and democratic republic, for the enjoyment of political freedom, social justice, individual and collective well-being and human solidarity.

China (excerpt) (1982)

CHINA IS ONE of the countries with the longest histories in the world. The people of all nationalities in China have jointly created a splendid culture and have a glorious revolutionary tradition.

Feudal China was gradually reduced after 1840 to a semi-colonial and semi-feudal country. ...

The People's Republic of China is a unitary multinational state built up jointly by the people of all its nationalities. Socialist relations of equality, unity and mutual assistance have been established among them and will continue to be strengthened. In the struggle to safeguard the unity of the nationalities, it is necessary to combat big-nation chauvinism, mainly Han chauvinism, and also necessary to combat local national chauvinism. The state does its utmost to promote the common prosperity of all nationalities in the country.

China's achievements in revolution and construction are inseparable from support by the people of the world. The future of China is closely linked with that of the whole world. China adheres to an independent foreign policy as well as to the five principles of mutual respect for sovereignty and territorial integrity, mutual nonaggression, non-interference in each other's internal affairs, equality and mutual benefit, and peaceful coexistence in developing diplomatic relations and economic and cultural exchanges with other countries; China consistently opposes imperialism, hegemonism, and colonialism, works to strengthen unity with the people of other countries, supports the oppressed nations and the developing countries in their just struggle to win and preserve national independence and develop their national economies, and strives to safeguard world peace and promote the cause of human progress.

This Constitution affirms the achievements of the struggles of the Chinese people of all nationalities and defines the basic system and basic tasks of the state in legal form; it is the fundamental law of the state and has supreme legal authority. The people of all nationalities, all state organs, the armed forces, all political parties and public organizations and all enterprises and undertakings in the country must take the Constitution as the basic norm of conduct, and they have the duty to uphold the dignity of the Constitution and ensure its implementation.

Republic of Korea (South Korea) (1987)

WE, THE PEOPLE of Korea, proud of a resplendent history and traditions dating from time immemorial,

  upholding the cause of the Provisional Republic of Korea Government born of the Independence Movement of 1 March 1919 and the democratic ideals of the uprising on 19 April 1960 against injustice,

  having assumed the mission of democratic reform and peaceful unification of our homeland and

  having determined to consolidate national unity with Justice, humanitarianism and brotherly love, and to destroy all social vices and injustice, and to afford equal opportunities to every person and provide for the fullest development of individual capabilities in all fields, including political, economic, social and cultural life by further strengthening the basic free and democratic order conducive to private initiative and public harmony, and to help each person discharge those duties and responsibilities concomitant to freedoms and rights, and to elevate the quality of life for all citizens and contribute to lasting world peace and the common prosperity of mankind and thereby to ensure security, liberty and happiness for ourselves and our posterity forever,

  do hereby amend, through national referendum following a resolution by the National Assembly, the Constitution, ordained and established on 12 July 1948, and amended eight times subsequently.

Democratic People's Republic of Korea (North Korea) (1998)

THE DEMOCRATIC PEOPLE'S Republic of Korea is a socialist fatherland of Juche which embodies the idea of and guidance by the great leader Comrade Kim Il Sung.

The great leader Comrade Kim Il Sung is the founder of the DPRK and the socialist Korea.

Comrade Kim Il Sung founded the immortal Juche idea, organized and guided an anti-Japanese revolutionary struggle under its banner, created revolutionary tradition, attained the historical cause of the national liberation, and founded the DPRK, built up a solid basis of construction of a sovereign and independent state in the fields of politics, economy, culture and military, and founded the DPRK.

Comrade Kim Il Sung put forward an independent revolutionary line, wisely guided the social revolution and construction at various levels, strengthened and developed the Republic into a people-centered socialist country and a socialist state of independence, self-sustenance, and self-defense.

Comrade Kim Il Sung clarified the fundamental principle of State building and activities, established the most superior state social system and political method, and social management system and method, and provided a firm basis for the prosperous and powerful socialist fatherland and the continuation of the task of completing the Juche revolutionary cause.

Comrade Kim Il Sung regarded "believing in the people as in heaven" as his motto, was always with the people, devoted his whole life to them, took care of and guided them with a noble politics of benevolence, and turned the whole society into one big and united family.

The great leader Comrade Kim Il Sung is the sun of the nation and the lodestar of the reunification of the fatherland. Comrade Kim Il Sung set the reunification of the country as the nation's supreme task, and devoted all his work and endeavors entirely to its realization.

Comrade Kim Il Sung, while turning the Republic into a mighty fortress for national reunification, indicated fundamental principles and methods for national reunification, developed the national reunification movement into a pan-national movement, and opened up a way for that cause, to be attained by the united strength of the entire nation.

The great leader Comrade Kim Il Sung made clear the fundamental idea of the Republic's external policy, expanded and developed diplomatic relations on this basis, and heightened the international prestige of the Republic. Comrade Kim Il Sung as a veteran world political leader, hew out a new era of independence, vigorously worked for the reinforcement and development of the socialist movement and the nonaligned movement, and for world peace and friendship between peoples, and made an immortal contribution to the mankind's independent cause.

Comrade Kim Il Sung was a genius ideological theoretician and a genius art leader, an ever-victorious, iron-willed brilliant commander, a great revolutionary and politician, and a great human being. Comrade Kim Il Sung's great idea and achievements in leadership are the eternal treasures of the nation and a fundamental guarantee for the prosperity and efflorescence of the DPRK.

The DPRK and the entire Korean people will uphold the great leader Comrade Kim Il Sung as the eternal President of the Republic, defend and carry forward his ideas and exploits and complete the Juche revolution under the leadership of the Workers' Party of Korea.

The DPRK Socialist Constitution is a Kim Il Sung constitution which legally embodies Comrade Kim Il Sung's Juche state construction ideology and achievements.

■ □ □ Some of the People Who Wrote the Constitution

WITH ITS ACCEPTANCE of the Potsdam Declaration in August 1945, Japan came under pressure to scrap the Meiji Constitution and enact a new Constitution. The Japanese authorities, however, were determined to preserve the national polity (i.e., the Imperial system) as a way of protecting the ruling class's privileges. Thus the draft created by the government's Constitutional Problem Investigation Committee (the Matsumoto Committee) came under fire as extremely conservative and a blatant attempt to preserve the status quo.

The headquarters of the Supreme Commander for the Allied Powers (SCAP), or GHQ, rejected this Matsumoto draft and directed its own Government Section to write a proposal. The current Constitution was drafted in only nine days – February 4 to February 11, 1946. The three items General Douglas MacArthur (SCAP) insisted be in the new Constitution were retention of the Emperor (as a constitutional monarch), renunciation of war, and the abolition of feudal institutions. With this framework, a 25-member team headed by Colonel Charles L. Kades, Deputy Chief of the Government Section, began work on the Constitution.

Because there was some friction between SCAP headquarters and the Far Eastern Commission (an 11-nation commission including the U.S., the U.K., the Soviet Union, and China established to advise SCAP GHQ) over the draft, it is worth including some of the views of some of the participants, researchers, and other people on the issue.

Sources were interviewed for the April 13, 1994, issue of *Views* published by Kodansha. Their comments appeared in Japanese and have been back-translated here, meaning that this text is a paraphrase.

Richard B. Finn
A Bluff to Preserve the Imperial System

UNDER-SECRETARY OF STATE Dean Acheson was for abolishing the Imperial System, and the pro-China, anti-Japan faction in the Department of State wanted to try the Emperor as a war criminal. But the occupation command felt retaining the Emperor would make it easier to govern Japan. They knew he would be useful. So even though they had no intention of deposing him, they told the Japanese people that they would abolish the Imperial system unless SCAP's Constitution was adopted.

Finn was born in 1917. He was a Japanese information officer with the U.S. Navy from 1942 to 1946. Served as legal officer with the Far Eastern Commission in 1946. Later served with the Department of State Japan desk and as professor emeritus at American University. Died in 1998.

Osborne Hauge
The U.S. Government Did Not Like Article 9

I WAS AMAZED when I heard about Article 9. This is something that MacArthur had cobbled together entirely on his own, and I wonder how much thought he really gave it. He was a brilliant man, but he was also conceited and strong-willed. There were a number of people on the drafting committees who argued that Article 9 was unrealistic given the international political situation, but MacArthur's word was law. You either went along or you got transferred out.

Washington did not like Article 9 either. They thought that it was unrealistic, that forcing this provision on Japan would mean the U.S. would have to be responsible for Japan's defense over the long term, and that it would end up costing U.S. taxpayers too much. We all assumed the occupation would be over in three to five years and Japan would have to be responsible for its own defense after that. We never dreamed U.S. forces would be stationed in Japan this long.

Hauge was born in 1913. He was a Navy Lieutenant Junior Grade in 1946. Was on the Legislative Committee responsible for Article 41 and other articles on the Diet. Having a journalistic background, he served as MacArthur's speechwriter.

Charles L. Kades
We Gave the Japanese a Great Constitution.
Now It's Up to Them.

JAPAN'S CONSTITUTION CONTAINS a very solid system of checks and balances among the three branches of government. The fact that collusion sometimes happens is not the Constitution's fault but is because the Japanese are not playing by the Constitution.

The Diet, for example, is fully empowered by the Constitution to exercise strong leadership. Some people complain the executive bureaucracy is more powerful than the politicians, but the problem here is the quality of politicians you get. If Japan had better politicians, things would not come to this pass. If you read what the Constitution says, it is clear that the Diet can control the bureaucracy.

Likewise, Japan's Supreme Court can be more activist in asserting its views. In fact, the Constitution gives the Japanese Supreme Court even more power than the U.S. Supreme Court has. It has, for example, more authority to declare legislation unconstitutional than the U.S. Supreme Court does. So it should be able to more rigorously ensure that each person's vote counts the same, among other principles. If it is not, the fault lies with the Supreme Court.

It is the same with local government. The Constitution gives local governments far more authority than they had under the Meiji Constitution. The governors have considerable leeway if they will take it. Instead, the local politicians all look to Tokyo for guidance, and that is why so much authority ends up concentrated at the national level. As things stand, the Tokyo bureaucracy has eviscerated local government. Japanese local politicians should be more independent.

Looking at Japan today, I think Japan has a great Constitution and I wish the people would use it.

Kades was born in 1906. Army Colonel and Deputy Chief of the Government Section at GHQ, he was responsible for the group drafting the Constitution and played an important role, including writing the renunciation of war (now Article 9) in the Preamble. Following retirement from the army, he practiced law until 1980. He died in 1996.

Theodore McNelly
MacArthur Thought of Article 9 Himself

COMMANDER ALFRED R. HUSSEY, JR., who was on the Steering Committee for the task force drafting the new Constitution and was responsible for the Preamble, said he wanted to give the Japanese a lesson in idealism. That is why the Preamble comes across as a bit preachy in parts. Japanese politicians and bureaucrats took offense at this, saying it read like an apology, but they ended up accepting it because we held the Imperial system hostage. Hussey basically did not like Japanese, and he did not even want to grant Japan the right to have the minimum necessary self-defense force. It was Col. Kades who made the decision to accept wording that could be interpreted as allowing for this bare-bones defense capability.

Article 9 is something that MacArthur himself thought of. But he presented it to the Japanese government as the will of the American government – and to the American government as something from Prime Minister Shidehara. On other occasions, he invoked the Emperor as its source, and elsewhere he claimed that the Japanese people wanted this provision included – all of this to blur his own responsibility for forcing Article 9 on Japan.

McNelly was born in 1919. Received his PhD from Columbia University. Majored in comparative politics and Japanese Constitutional law. Served as research analyst with the Far Eastern Commission Public Information Office 1946 to 1948. Later held other posts, including University of Maryland professor emeritus. A leading U.S. authority on Japanese Constitutional law and author of numerous texts, including "Induced Revolution: The Policy and Process of Constitutional Reform in Occupied Japan" in *Democratizing Japan. The Allied Occupation* (1987) and *Politics and Government in Japan* (1992).

Richard A. Poole
Who Decided the Emperor Should Be a Symbol?

THE FIRST ISSUE I dealt with after getting to Japan was the territorial issue. This was in 1945, and it was Col. Kades who okayed ceding two of the northern islands to the Soviets. He was not very favorably inclined toward Japan. In this same vein, he wanted to make it almost impossible for Japan to amend its new Constitution by requiring a three-quarters affirmative vote in the Diet. We argued that that was too extreme and finally settled on two thirds. Even so, this is still a very high hurdle that makes it difficult to amend the Constitution.

We wrote the new Constitution in just a week. Because MacArthur did not want the Japanese to write the draft of the new Constitution, he decided we should get there first. So we did. It was a rush, but we did. It really floored us when he gave the order in February 1946 to draft a new Constitution in one week. We were basically military people. Sure, there were some lawyers in the group, but not a single Constitutional expert. It was an amateur production that slapped the Constitution together in just one week, so I can understand how some people might want to amend the thing. In fact, I'm amazed it has not been changed yet.

The Emperor was useful to the Occupation forces. He is the one who called for an end to the war in his August 15 broadcast, and both his renunciation of divinity and his cooperative attitude toward the new Constitution made him much more useful than the reactionary nobility. So we decided to keep the Imperial system, but I do not really remember whose idea it was to make him a symbol. At one of the conferences, somebody suggested, "Why don't we just call him a symbol?" and everyone else seconded the idea.

When I first heard about Article 9, I told the group I thought it would be better not to include such an unrealistic idea in the Constitution. But Col. Kades said, "This is an order from the top." And since he was the emissary from MacArthur, our hands were tied.

Poole was born in 1919 in Yokohama. His great-great-grandfather had been U.S. Consul General in Hakodate. Joined Department of State in 1941 and served as Consul General in Montreal and Barcelona. Worked on foreign affairs in GHQ Government Section. Served on the Committee on the Emperor, Treaties, and Enabling Provisions and was responsible for Chapter I on the Emperor. Following occupation duty, served many years with the Department of State.

Chronology

From the End of World War II
to the Promulgation of the Constitution

1945   July 26   U.S., U.K., and China announce the Potsdam
Declaration

August 30   Supreme Commander for Allied Powers Douglas
MacArthur arrives at Atsugi

October 4   MacArthur suggests former Prime Minister Konoye
Fumimaro revise the Constitution

October 9   Shidehara Kijuuro replaces Prince Higashikuni
Naruhiko as Prime Minister

October 11   MacArthur issues five democratization directives to
Shidehara Cabinet

October 25   Constitutional Problems Investigation Committee
(Matsumoto Committee) empaneled with Matsumoto
Jouji as chair

November 22   Konoye presents his draft of amended Meiji
Constitution to the Emperor

December 8   Matsumoto announces his four principles for
Constitutional reform, including retaining Imperial
rule basically unchanged and building in broader
protections for human rights and freedom

December 26   Matsumoto Committee announces its draft

December 27   Far Eastern Commission is established

1946   January 1   Emperor issues statement renouncing his divinity

February 1   Mainichi newspaper runs scoop detailing the
Matsumoto Committee draft

February 3   MacArthur indicates his three principles and orders
Government Section to come up with a GHQ draft

February 8   Japanese government presents gist of Matsumoto draft
to GHQ

February 13   GHQ rejects Matsumoto draft and gives Japanese
government GHQ draft

February 22   Shidehara Cabinet decides to accept GHQ draft

March 6   Japanese government announces draft for revised
Constitution

May 22   Yoshida Shigeru becomes Prime Minister

June 20   Draft of revised Constitution is presented
to 90th Session of Imperial Diet

November 3   Constitution promulgated
(to go into effect May 3, 1947)

Timeline of the Process Leading to the Current Constitution's Promulgation

APRIL 17, 1946 Announcement of the draft revised Constitution
First Yoshida Cabinet took office on May 22
with Minister of State Kanamori Tokujirou
assigned chief responsibility for shepherding the new
Constitution through the Diet

MAY 27 Draft referred to the Privy Council
Approved by the full session

JUNE 25 Draft sent to the House of Representatives

JUNE 28 Referred to the House of Representatives
Committee on the Constitution Revision Bill
Committee approved draft with some changes

AUGUST 24 Draft approved by the House of Representatives
421 in favor, 8 opposed

AUGUST 26 Draft sent to the House of Peers

AUGUST 30 Referred to the House of Peers
Special Committee on the Constitution Revision Bill
Subcommittee formed to consider amendments
Some amendments considered
*Draft approved by Special Committee
on the Constitution Revision Bill*

OCTOBER 6 Draft approved by the House of Peers
Majority in favor

OCTOBER 7 Draft approved by the House of Representatives
Overwhelming majority in favor

OCTOBER 12 Sent back to the Privy Council
*Unanimously approved (with two members absent)
Sent to the Emperor for final decision*

NOVEMBER 3 Constitution promulgated

■ □ □ Procedure for Amending the Constitution

THERE HAS LATELY been much talk of Constitutional reform, and a number of differently nuanced terms have been suggested to describe this process; they include amending the Constitution, augmenting the Constitution by adding new provisions, and creating a new Constitution. Yet even though politicians of all persuasions are discussing what should be added and what should be deleted, in a debate that has spread well beyond the formal sessions in and around the Diet, the actual process and procedures to be followed if and when it is finally decided to change the Constitution are themselves still very much up in the air. Thus we talked with leading politicians, bureaucrats, and other experts to ferret out the legal framework and literature and to shed some light on the actual procedure for amending the Constitution if and when that occurs.

Why has this issue come up now?

This is not, of course, the first time that people have said the Constitution needs to be rethought and have put forth suggestions. Yet past discussions have always withered in the face of opposition from the Constitution's defenders and the weight of negative public opinion, and there has been no real debate to date on Constitutional reform. This time is different. One difference is that there has been a sea change in public opinion. Polls by the *Asahi* newspaper and other media organizations now consistently show over half of the respondents in favor of amending the Constitution.

Even more important, Prime Minister Koizumi Jun'ichirou has been much more outspoken on the Constitution than his predecessors had been. Among his notable comments are:

"It would be easy to marshal support for amending the Constitution if it were only to provide for the direct election of the Prime Minister."

– statement at his press conference upon taking office in April 2001

"[Amending the Constitution to provide for direct election of the Prime Minister] would clarify the procedures for amending the Constitution."

– ibid.

"While it would be a good idea to amend the Constitution to allow Japan to exercise the right of collective defense, barring that, the priority has to be on Japan-U.S. friendship and the Security Treaty. I intend to abide by the Constitution as currently interpreted, but we also need to plan for every contingency."

– ibid.

"(The Constitution) is not writ in stone. As public opinion evolves, we need to give the idea of amending the Constitution careful consideration when the time comes."

– remarks to the House of Councillors in May 2001

"The best way (to provide for the exercise of the right of collective defense) would be to amend the Constitution so that there is no misunderstanding."

– remarks to the House of Representatives in May 2001

"There is a lot wrong (with the current Constitution). Article 9, for example."

– remarks to the House of Representatives Special Committee on Legislation to Provide Means to Deal with Emergencies in May 2002

"I can understand why some people may think a Constitution that has not changed for over 50 years is out of date, and I think it would be good to be more flexible and to make the necessary changes."

– ibid.

"Given that the SDF are constituted to fend off foreign aggressors, other countries naturally think of the SDF as a military. Yet because of our Constitutional restraints, we do not call them a military force. So some people say this is unnatural and we should take another look at the Constitution."

– ibid.

"I would like to work on an LDP draft that could be ready by November 2005 in time for the 50th anniversary of the LDP's founding."

– August 2003

"There is a lot of ambiguity in the Constitution. This is not just limited to Article 9. For example, Article 89's prohibition on using public moneys for charitable or educational purposes is also counter-intuitive. Likewise, Article 43 says that the members of the Diet should be elected by all of the people, but we have the anomaly of candidates (for the House of Representatives) who fail to be elected from single-representative districts but are elected on the proportional representation rolls. This defies common sense."

– ibid.

These comments by the Prime Minister have in turn provoked greater activity on this issue in the Liberal Democratic Party (LDP), the Democratic Party of Japan (DPJ), and the Cross-party Parliamentarian Research Committee on the Constitution. Even before Koizumi was elected Prime Minister, Research Commissions on the Constitution were established in the House of Representatives and House of Councillors in January 2001, following which the Cross-party Parliamentarian Research Committee on the Constitution drafted its Bill for a National Referendum on Amending the Constitution in November 2001, the DPJ's Constitution Research Committee issued its interim report in December 2001, the House of Representatives' Research Commission on the Constitution issued its interim report in November 2002, and the LDP and Komei Party (KMP) established a consultative committee in April 2004 to discuss the enactment of legislation to provide for a national referendum. These are just a few of the many signs of activity on the issue of amending the Constitution. Yet even so, all of these efforts are still interim and ongoing, and the situation is very much in flux. Notwithstanding, there is a very real likelihood that more specific action will be taken following the release of the LDP draft in November 2005.

With Prime Minister Koizumi's comments at the vortex, there has been a whirlwind of advocacy by political parties, Diet committees, and the private sector calling for amending the Constitution. Yet many of these calls have been in the abstract – efforts to create a mood that threatens to sweep aside discussion of specifics. And this has in turn sparked counter-calls and considerable discussion of details to see if, indeed, amendment is warranted.

The key role played by political parties

While the Constitution does have provision for amendment – Article 96 stating that the Diet shall initiate it and outlining the other procedural requirements – it does not go into much detail on the actual mechanics of this process. As a result, a number of problems are likely to emerge at every step of the way, as has been pointed out by the House of Representatives and House of Councillors Research Commissions on the Constitution, the Cross-party Parliamentarian Research Committee, and the internal study groups established by the political parties.

One of the problems that everyone has noticed is the question of who would propose a Constitutional amendment in the Diet. While the Constitution is, to borrow Article 98's wording, "the supreme law of the nation," it is a law like any other. Thus while it seems clear that Diet members, acting as representatives of the people, can move to amend it in the Diet, most other bills, including bills to amend existing laws, are submitted to the Diet by the executive branch. At present, approximately two thirds of all bills submitted to the Diet are submitted by the Cabinet office. Does it follow then that a bill to amend the Constitution may also be submitted to the Diet by the Cabinet?

The consensus seems to argue against this and to take a more literal interpretation of Article 96's "shall be initiated by the Diet" to argue that the initiative here cannot be taken by the Cabinet and has to come from within the Diet. Yet at the same time, seeming to counter this, Article 72 states: "The Prime Minister, representing the Cabinet, submits bills, reports on general national affairs and foreign relations to the Diet and exercises control and supervision over various administrative branches." Following from this, there are those who argue that the Prime Minister, representing the Cabinet, can submit a bill for the amendment of the Constitution. This issue has yet to be resolved.

Article 96 of the Constitution reads in part:

Amendments to this Constitution shall be initiated by the Diet, through a concurring vote of two-thirds or more of all the members of each House and shall thereupon be submitted to the people for ratification, which shall require the affirmative vote of a majority of all votes cast thereon, at a special referendum or at such election as the Diet shall specify.

Thus even though people talk of amending the Constitution as a single, simple process, there are differences of opinion even on how and where this process should start. And there are many other procedural issues that are even more confounding.

Article 96's Depiction of the Amendment Process

HOUSE OF REPRESENTATIVES

⅔ *approval*

HOUSE OF COUNCILLORS

⅔ *approval*

↓

Proposal

↓

National Referendum

(*majority affirmative*)

↓

Promulgation of Amended Constitution

Strategic shift of focus

So far, discussion of amending the Constitution has focused on whether Article 9 or other specific articles should be amended or not. Yet there is increasing recognition of the need to also focus on the procedural issues and on how amending the Constitution would actually work. As part of this, there has been considerable discussion of a national referendum law.

A national referendum on amending the Constitution would have to take place after both Houses of the Diet agreed by at least two-thirds majorities on an amendment proposal. Who would be eligible to vote? How would they vote? Who would decide the date of the referendum? How would the votes be counted? How would the result be determined? And more. All of these details need to be set forth in a national referendum law. Yet there is no national referendum law in place at this point that could be invoked for amending the Constitution. Thus there are those who, putting the actual proposal to be voted on aside, want to work first on drafting referendum legislation.

This shift of focus from advocating specific amendments to putting the referendum mechanism in place marks a strategic shift by the LDP and government advocates of amendment. Even though recent opinion polls have showed more then 50% of respondents in favor of amending the Constitution, advocates still anticipate fierce resistance should they to try to rush amendment through. Thus they have created this technical separation between the campaign to amend the Constitution and the campaign to pass a national referendum law and are concentrating, for the time being, on enacting a national referendum law. And because the national referendum law would be an ordinary law like any other, it should be possible to draft it and enact it just like any other law (i.e., with a simple majority in both Houses). Yet if we accept the idea that the people are sovereign, we cannot afford to ignore this stealth campaign that is taking place to out-flank the popular will.

Main points in a national referendum law

The two main points needing examination in this national referendum law are (1) the referendum procedure and (2) how "a majority of all votes cast thereon" is to be defined.

On the referendum modality itself, it would be possible to have a ballot that asks the people to vote on each amendment separately or to have a ballot that does not offer this breakdown but simply asks the people to vote on the final package as a whole. In the "breakdown ballot" formula, if there were plural amendments being offered for consideration, each would be listed separately and voters would be asked to vote yes or no on each. This would allow the maximum exercise of voter discretion. By contrast, the "package ballot" formula would propose the new Constitution with all of the proposed amendments in place and would ask voters to vote yes or no on the whole. There would be very little room for the exercise of voter discretion.

At present, the national referendum law draft that the LDP and KMP are considering is based upon the Bill for a National Referendum on Amending the Constitution produced in November 2001 by the Cross-party Parliamentarian Research Committee on the Constitution chaired by Nakayama Tarou. This bill simply states that "if the proposal approved by the Diet has separate provisions for each of the places to be amended and is proposed to the people that way, then the people should vote on each of the amendments as proposed." It adds: "This issue can be resolved by the Diet in how it formulates its proposal," thus avoiding any clear statement on which formula is preferable.

Yet because this national referendum is an essential part of the provision and the results must reflect the popular will, the question of how the proposal is to be formulated and the vote to be held will become a major subject of debate as the discussion progresses.

On the question of defining how the votes cast in a referendum are to be defined, Article 96 simply specifies that approval requires "the affirmative vote of a majority of all votes cast thereon." There is no provision on the scope. And looking simply at the wording that is there, it would seem that all citizens (from mere infants to centenarians) would be eligible to vote.

More realistically, it is assumed that this means all of the people with the right to vote, which is basically anyone aged 20 or above. But this still leaves the question of whether a majority of all eligible voters is needed or if approval simply requires a majority of the people who actually vote. The assumption is that it only a majority of the votes cast that is required. The proposal by the Cross-party Parliamentarian Research Committee on the Constitution further restricts this by saying "a majority of all valid votes cast." In essence, the issue is a question of how to define the denominator – the number at least half of which is needed – and this is bound to be a major point of contention given the differences between the Constitution's defenders and amendment's advocates. It would also, for example, be possible to argue for an age cap on the eligible voter population. Likewise, although there is no mention of voter turnout for a national referendum, there is bound to be heated debate over the question of whether or not the results of a referendum that draws poor voter turnout truly reflect the popular will.

Other issues in the Bill for a National Referendum on Amending the Constitution include the time interval between the Diet's putting the referendum proposal to the people and the actual voting, restrictions on media reporting, and a prohibition against campaigning by non-Japanese. All of these provisions are bound to be profoundly controversial. Accordingly, the bill for the national referendum is drawing at least as much scrutiny as the actual amendment proposals themselves, and it is expected this will be a very heated part of the battle over Constitution amendment.

In June 2004, the LDP and KMP established a two-party ruling coalition council to consult on referendum specifics and to submit a bill to the FY2004 ordinary session of the Diet. However, no bill was ready by the time the session ended. Nonetheless, the LDP wants to submit a bill to the FY2005 ordinary session, and everyone is watching anxiously to see whether one will actually be submitted or not, and if one is, what it will be.

Incremental amendment versus all-at-once amendment

One of the main reasons the Constitution has not been amended in the nearly 60 years since its promulgation is that the barriers to amendment are so high. Not only are two-thirds affirmatives needed in both Houses of the Diet, majority approval in a subsequent national referendum is also required.

So far, the main thrust of the push to amend the Constitution has been to enumerate the many things that critics say need to be changed – the Preamble, Article 1, Article 9, Article 89, and other articles as well as references to Japanese culture and history and the use of the Japanese language and wording – and to advocate all-at-once amendment taking care of all of these problems in one fell swoop. On the other side, however, have been the incrementalists who say the first priority should be to make it easier to amend the Constitution and that these other specific issues can wait. In effect, these people advocate amendment as prelude to further amendment. Yet this is a patently specious argument from the popular sovereignty standpoint.

The cynic would argue that such incrementalists want to package an amendment making the Constitution easier to amend with a few other changes such as specifying environmental rights and privacy rights – things on which there is broad popular consensus and that it would be hard to vote against – and use this opening shot as a wedge to open the floodgates to further amendment. Should this initial proposal be approved, the next stage would be to take advantage of the amendment-friendly provision to repeal Article 9, curtail individual freedoms, and ram through other changes that do not have widespread popular support. In short, the worry is that the incrementalist approach is simply an attempt by the state to write a more convenient Constitution.

Is amendment possible?

Any simulation of the effort by the government and the ruling coalition to amend the Constitution has to take into account what might be done to win over or at least neutralize the opposition. As noted above, any amendment to the Constitution must win the approval of at least two thirds of both Houses of the Diet before it can even be put to the people. As of this writing, this would mean approval by at least 321 Representatives and 162 Councillors. As of the end of July 2004, the ruling LDP-KMP coalition had 283 seats in the House of Representatives and 139 in the House of Councillors. This is not enough. If the Constitution is to be amended, the coalition will have to win over the opposition, especially the DPJ.

It is said that there are many DPJ Diet members who are even more pro-amendment than the LDP is, and that many DPJ members would surely join a non-partisan parliamentary coalition to amend the Constitution. Thus while it would have been inconceivable that the LDP could have co-opted substantial numbers of JSP members to the pro-amendment fold under the old "1955 structure" when the political axis pitted the LDP against the JSP, the emergence of the DPJ has fundamentally altered the political equation.

Adding the ruling coalition (LDP and KMP) and DPJ seats would give amendment approximately 96% of the House of Representatives and approximately 91% of the House of Councillors. Even just the cooperation of only 37 of the DPJ House of Representatives members and 23 of its House of Councillors members would still give the pro-amendment forces the two thirds they need to pass a proposal and put it to the people. While these figures may seem high or low depending upon how you read the situation, given that the gap between the LDP and the DPJ is not as ideologically partisan as that between the LDP and the JSP was, it is not inconceivable that a motion to amend the Constitution could win the necessary two-thirds approvals in both Houses of the Diet.

Yet it should also be noted that the DPJ includes a large number of members who came of age in the JSP and are fervently opposed to tampering with the Constitution, meaning that Constitution amendment would be extremely

Distribution of Seats in the Diet (as of end July 2004)

	HOUSE OF REPRESENTATIVES	HOUSE OF COUNCILLORS
LDP	249	115
KMP	34	24
DPJ	178	82
JCP	9	9
SDP	6	5
INDEPENDENTS	4	7
TOTAL	480	242

divisive within the party. At the same time, there are also many doves within the LDP who see no need to rush to amend the Constitution, and it is impossible to tell what these people might do.

Will the LDP and DPJ join forces?

Were the LDP and the DPJ to work together on Constitution reform, this would entail three-party talks with the LDP and KMP on one side and the DPJ on the other – thus assuming the establishment of some three-party consultative mechanism involving the three parties across the aisle. From their public statements, both the LDP and the DPJ appear to be positively inclined toward amending the Constitution, the LDP having said "we hope to put an LDP proposal to amend the Constitution together in 2005 as one fitting way to commemorate the 50th anniversary of the party's founding" and the DPJ having said "we want to put a proposal for amending the Constitution together by the 60th anniversary of the Constitution's promulgation – in 2006." Thus it would come as no surprise were such a consultative mechanism to be established to discuss Constitution reform. That said, there are readily apparent differences in the two parties' approaches to the actual provisions. On Article 9, for example, the LDP's "Talking Points on Constitutional Reform" says "it would be folly to assume world peace can be achieved simply by publicizing Article 9;" the DPJ's "Interim Report on the Constitution" says "we should continue to publicize the Constitution of Japan and Article 9's pacifism both at home and abroad." The LDP, DPJ, and KMP may agree on the general desirability of amending the Constitution, but that does not mean they are agreed on the specific amendments to be pushed, and the discussion is likely to turn acrimonious when it gets down to specifics.

Linked to this jockeying among the parties is the possibility that special committees may be constituted to discuss Constitution reform in the House of Representatives and the House of Councillors. Traditionally, special committees have been established to focus deliberations within the Diet. Examples range from those constituted to expedite consideration of specific areas such as emergency-response contingency legislation, tax policy, and political reform to those constituted to deal with politically sensitive scandals involving prominent political figures (such as the Sagawa Kyubin scandal of 1992 and the *juusen*-meltdown scandal of the mid-1990s).

Although special committees were established in both Houses of the Diet in 1957 to look at Constitution reform, the JSP refused to take part in either of these special committees and they were subsequently disbanded in 1965. Later, special committees on the Constitution were established in both Houses commemorating the Constitution's 50th anniversary, and these committees are scheduled to issue final reports by January 2005 or so. However, because these Special Committees sought opposition participation (from the DPJ and JCP), they have necessarily had to take neutral stances and were not empowered to submit legislative bills to the Diet. As a result, voices were heard at the plenary session of the Cross-party Parliamentarian Research Committee on the Constitution in favor of creating standing committees on the Constitution that would be empowered to draft and submit bills, and moves are now afoot to establish such standing committees. As might be expected, many of the people in favor of the standing committees are also in favor of amending the Constitution.

What would Diet debate on amending the Constitution look like?

While research commissions and cross-party parliamentarian committees with no authority to submit legislation for Diet deliberation cannot in themselves amend the Constitution, the establishment of committees, either special or standing, with the authority to draft legislation for submission to the full Diet would mark a major step forward on the path to amending the Constitution. It is thus worth considering how actual Diet deliberations might play out.

The current Constitution is silent on what kind of deliberative process would be needed. And because the issue is one of amending the Constitution, it is possible that this might be subject to detailed regulation as a special case under the National Diet Law (which stipulates the internal workings of the House of Representatives and House of Councillors).

Yet such deliberative procedures often follow precedent, and the precedent here is that provided by the amendment of the Meiji Constitution of 1889 to transform it into the current Constitution.

Because the current Constitution is technically an amendment of the Meiji Constitution, its enactment followed the relevant provisions of Article 73 of that Constitution. That Article required that at least two thirds of the members of both Houses be present and that at least two thirds of the members present vote in favor of any amendment for it to pass. The provisions of Article 96 of the current Constitution are similar.

Assuming the current Constitution is amended following this process, there will be no real need for the same house of the Diet to deliberate and pass the amendment proposition twice. (Of course, that could change if the House of Councillors rejects the version that the House of Representatives passes, in which case the House of Representatives would be asked to consider the proposal again.) Yet when the present Constitution was adopted, the House of Representatives deliberated and adopted the amended Constitution; this adopted version was then sent to the House of Peers, where it was deliberated and adopted by the full house, and it was then sent back to the House of Representatives for deliberation and final adoption, so that the House of Representatives did pass it twice. As such, there is a strong likelihood that the House of Representatives would be asked to pass the same proposal twice for amending the current Constitution. And indeed, having the House of Representatives have the final say after the proposal is passed by the House of Councillors seems appropriate in light of the House of Representatives' dominant position.

Article 73 of the Meiji Constitution

When it has become necessary in future to amend the provisions of the present Constitution, a project to that effect shall be submitted to the Imperial Diet by Imperial Order.

2. In the above case, neither House can open the debate, unless not less than two-thirds of the whole number of Members are present, and no amendment can be passed, unless a majority of not less than two-thirds of the Members present is obtained.

How would the national referendum be conducted?

As noted above, the details of this national referendum have yet to be worked out by the Diet. This will be done as it deliberates the national referendum law.

As such, the discussion here is based upon the Bill for a National Referendum on Amending the Constitution as drafted by the Cross-party Parliamentarian Research Committee on the Constitution and looks only at the flow from the time the Diet makes the proposal until the amended Constitution is promulgated. There are basically six points at issue:

The referendum date: Probably 60-90 days after the Diet makes its proposal.

The voting method: This will be one vote per person. The proposal will be stated and voters will be asked to indicate whether they are for it or against it, "for" indicated by ○ and "against" by ×. (Note, however, that it is not yet clear what the procedure would be if there were multiple amendments proposed separately to be voted up or down separately.)

Administering the national referendum: This would be done by a national election board.

Counting the votes: This would follow the procedure used for counting votes for the proportional representation part of the House of Representatives election.

Tallying the results: It is assumed that ballots left blank or marked with anything except ○ or × would be declared invalid. If that happens, only the yeas and nays would be counted and one side or the other would necessarily have a majority.

Informing the public: The Prime Minister, national election board, prefectural and local election boards, and everyone else would be responsible for ensuring that the people are fully informed of the referendum procedure and such other details as necessary.

In addition, the referendum law would have to provide for suits contesting the referendum results to be filed within 30 days, and it has to be assumed there would also be appeals to the higher courts and then the Supreme Court. Thus it is important to clarify ahead of time what, if any, restrictions should be placed on campaigning for or against the referendum, as well as what, if any, restrictions should be placed on the media and on campaigning by non-Japanese.

If a referendum is held, it is likely that everyone will choose a side and the country will be divided between those in favor of amending the Constitution and those against. It can be further assumed that everyone in both camps will do everything possible to mobilize the media to win converts. It is thus very likely that this would turn into a major battle involving all of the media. Will this battle be no-holds-barred or will there be rules of engagement? In an ordinary election, the Prime Minister often appears in campaign advertising. Would this be allowed in the event of a national referendum? What about the use of celebrities and endorsements?

From promulgation to implementation

If the majority of the (valid) votes cast in the national referendum were in favor of the proposed Constitution as amended, the Prime Minister would immediately move to initiate procedures for the new Constitution's promulgation.

Under Article 96, paragraph 2, of the Constitution, "Amendments when so ratified shall immediately be promulgated by the Emperor in the name of the people as an integral part of this Constitution." As such, it is assumed that the Emperor would promulgate the new Constitution to the House of Councillors, as was done for the current Constitution. Although there is no stipulation as to when the new Constitution would actually take effect, and this might well depend upon how extensively it is amended, it is assumed this would be announced at the same time.

As a result, immediately upon promulgation, all of the ministries, agencies, and other government bodies would set to work checking to see if the laws and regulations enacted under the current (pre-amendment) Constitution are compatible with the new Constitution. And because there would obviously be incompatibilities, these would need to be rectified by amending the relevant laws and regulations – a process that would have to entail the drafting of amendments and their consideration by the Diet. Depending upon how extensively the Constitution is amended, this could well be a massive task involving the amendment of many, many laws and regulations. Some people have speculated, for example, that if the provisions having to do with local government are amended – and this is an area that has been cited as needing clarification – the majority of the laws and regulations covering local government would need to be amended accordingly. In addition, innumerable government documents would have to be revised, and this could well turn out to be an even bigger job than the 2001 streamlining of the executive bureaucracy – with commensurate impact on all aspects of Japanese life.

■□□

Even though people speak of amending the Constitution as though it were a simple process, it is actually a quite complex and immense operation involving study of each of the articles to be amended, deliberation in the Diet, a national referendum, promulgation, and then all of the coordination to implementation. And of course this process would be further complicated by jockeying within and among the major political parties. The DPJ is particularly problematic, since the majority of its Diet members are against amending the Constitution and it will be very difficult for the party as a whole to agree. However, this is not to say things would be smooth sailing even for the LDP. Just because someone is an LDP Diet member does not mean he or she is automatically in favor of amending the Constitution. And the smaller Social Democratic Party (SDP) and Japan Communist Party (JCP) could be expected to do everything they can to derail the amendment campaign and to keep the Constitution as it is.

Given the potential hazards, this is not something to be undertaken lightly. If it is promoted by the politicians purely for partisan purposes, ignoring the fact that sovereignty ultimately rests with the people, it could well turn out to be an empty exercise meaning no more than extra hours of overtime for hard-worked bureaucrats and extra documentation press runs for the government printing office.

– The Constitution of Japan Project 2004 Team

Expected Timeline for Amending the Current Constitution

Submission of bill to amend the Constitution to the House of Representatives

Submitted by executive branch?
Submitted by ruling party(ies)?
Submitted by ruling and opposition parties in concert?

→ Establishment of (Special) Committee on the Constitution in the House of Representatives

DELIBERATION AND PASSAGE
Unclear if adoption by committee would require ⅔
Start of deliberations in Diet on amending the Constitution

→ Adoption by full House of Representatives

Would this require ⅔ of all members?
Unclear if full House of Representatives adoption takes place at this point. However, this is the point at which full House of Representatives approval took place in amending the Meiji Constitution.

→ Establishment of (Special) Committee on the Constitution in the House of Councillors

DELIBERATION AND PASSAGE
Unclear if adoption by Committee would require ⅔
Deliberation in the House of Councillors starts after the end of House of Representatives deliberations?

→ Adoption by full House of Councillors

Would this require ⅔ of all members?

→ Adoption by full House of Representatives

Would this require ⅔ of all members?
Unclear if House of Representatives has to adopt draft twice.
Yet House of Representatives passed the bill a second time at this point when amending the Meiji Constitution.

→ **Diet proposes Constitutional amendment for national referendum**

> *Requires ⅔ approval of both houses.*
> *If procedure follows the recommendation of the*
> *LDP and KMP's report by the core people within the Ruling*
> *Parties Consultative Committee on National Referendum, etc.,*
> *there would be a joint proposal for Constitution amendment*
> *issued by the Speaker of the House of Representatives and the*
> *President of the House of Councillors.*

Expected Timeline from the Diet to Promulgation

Proposal of the amended Constitution

BY THE PRIME MINISTER
Referendum to be held 60–90 days later
↓

Cabinet
↓

National referendum

Majority (of valid votes) opposed → REJECTED
Majority (of valid votes) in favor → ADOPTED
↓

New Constitution promulgated

How to ensure all people are aware of results?
How to ensure all laws and regulations are compatible
with the new Constitution?
↓

New Constitution goes into effect

□■□ Some Japanese Views

Individuals

□■□ The Constitution Is Not the Problem

Anno Moyoko

Anno Moyoko is a manga artist.

Born in 1971. Debuted with *Bessatsu Friend Juliet* (Kodansha) upon graduation from high school. Has been prolific with megahits, including *Choukanden Shoujo Mona* (Electrifying Lass Mona) (Kodansha), *Happy Mania* (Shoudensha), *Shibou to Iu Na no Fuku wo Kite* (Wearing a Suit of Fat) (Shufu to Seikatsu-sha), and *Flowers and Bees, Sakuran, Sugar Sugar Rune,* and the *Beauty Magazine* series (all Kodansha).

I AM REALLY kicking myself for agreeing to write something on the Constitution. The last time I read the Constitution was for a class many years ago. When was that? In elementary school? In junior high school? We had a copy around somewhere around the house – a big-print edition in an easy-to-read book that my parents bought – but it was not something I ever read. For 20 years, I have lived oblivious of the Constitution.

Which is to say it has been possible for me to live these last 20 years without encountering a single phrase or clause from the Constitution. Of course, I know adults are supposed to be more responsible and conscientious and all, but it is possible to go through life in Japan without ever thinking about this. Maybe there is something wrong with me. Maybe it is Japan that is the problem.

But of course, here I am shirking responsibility for my own ignorance and trying to blame this nebulous entity we call Japan. And it is this utter unwillingness to feel responsible – this feeling that this is all so other-worldly – that I feel about myself as I prepare to confront the Constitution.

One of the things everyone harps on in discussing the Constitution is fundamental human rights. I don't know if people's rights are protected in crime cases or not, but I get the feeling there is no real respect at all for human rights in ordinary Japanese life. The whole idea is a shambles. We talk about *ijime* (bullying) in schools, but this same wanton unwillingness to accept individuals as real people deserving dignity and respect is rampant at work and throughout society. Even in the home.

Even as the schools ignore *ijime*, they arrange intramural athletic events so there are no winners or losers. And everyone is supposed to treat the teachers as best friends. This is supposed to be a great show of equality. Surely they cannot be serious, I think. It is mind-boggling. I have immense trouble with the idea that respecting fundamental human rights means everyone has to be the same and equal in all ways.

Not long ago, a woman somewhat younger than myself saw I was carrying an expensive handbag. It was a bag she liked, and she envied me for having it. So far no problem. But then she started screaming and carrying on: "She cheated. How come Anno's the only one who can buy that bag? It's not fair!" I try to ignore drunken ravings, but this was worse than drunk. This was a basic mindset disorder. And it really pissed me off.

I did not cheat. There was nothing underhanded about this at all. I worked long and hard to create good manga. I earned my fees. And I used my hard-earned money to buy the bag. In fact, I did more than work long and hard to create that manga. I also worked long and hard to get to the point where I could do this. None of it has been easy. And it is only right – only natural – that someone who has not been through this and who can only bitch and moan should not be able to buy the same bag. There's nothing unfair about it. It is as fair as fair can be.

But this idea of fair reward for good work seems to be missing from the Japanese idea of "fair and equal." Instead, everyone's entitled. And the media encourage this nonsense. Things have gotten so bad I sometimes half-wonder if we should not reinstate some kind of caste system.

The Constitution itself proposes the most reasonable and trouble-free course: equal opportunity. Yet Japanese society completely ignores the Constitution and expects equal outcomes. Before we start making all kinds of proposals for what the Constitution should or should not say, we should take a good look at what it actually does say. Instead, I get the feeling that our everyday lives are far removed from the Constitution's wording and spirit.

The Constitution is like a box that just has form and shape but is empty of substance. We need to fill this box with the spirit of what real people really think, feel, and do. For without that, no matter how impressive its outward appearance may be, it will still be without meaning.

I mentioned *ijime*. This bullying, tormenting, and virtual enslavement of *ijime*'s victims is clearly a violation of Article 18's provision that "no person shall be held in bondage of any kind." People who are subject to *ijime* are forced to live their lives in a kind of bondage, but the people inflicting the *ijime* go scot-free. Even when the poor person is driven to suicide or suffers fatal injuries as a result of the *ijime*, there is no real punishment for the perpetrators if they are minors. Of course, there will be people who object that I am focusing on a very minor detail, but this is a prime example: something is terribly wrong in Japan.

And I do not see how rewriting the Constitution is going to fix anything. If we have gotten things this wrong even with an idealistic Constitution, I shudder to think what will happen with a new, "realist" Constitution. The box is not the problem. It is us. It is society. And that is why we need to be able to sit down and think about the Constitution and what it means for our lives. It will not be easy, but it is an essential first step.

☐■☐ Popular Sovereignty vs. the Japanese Reality

Hasegawa Michiko

Hasegawa Michiko is Professor, Saitama University Faculty of Liberal Arts. Born in 1946. Graduated from the University of Tokyo Faculty of Letters Department of Philosophy and Religion. Completed the doctoral course at University of Tokyo. Among her works are *Kara Kokoro* (Open Mind) and *Baberu no Nazo: Yahauisuto no Bouken* (The Puzzle of Babel: the Yahwist Challenge) (both from Chuuou Kouronsha), *Seigi no Soushitsu: Han-jidaiteki Kousatu* (The Loss of Justice: Anti-contemporary Observations) (PHP), and the co-authored *Kuni no Kokoro, Kuni no Katachi* (The Heart of the Country, the Shape of the Country) (Fusousha).

EVERYONE KNOWS THAT popular sovereignty is one of the most important principles underlying the Japanese Constitution. We are taught as early as elementary school that popular sovereignty, the guarantee of fundamental human rights, and our commitment to peace are the Constitution's three core concepts. But if you push a bit and ask people to define popular sovereignty, you find this is surprisingly difficult for most people.

One typical junior high school civics textbook defines popular sovereignty as: "The people are the ultimate political authority in the state and it is the people who govern." This certainly is not incorrect, but it by no means gives us a clear understanding of the concept. The statement that "the people" are the ultimate political authority, for example, is almost meaningless because all of us are "the people." In fact, "popular sovereignty" means nothing unless and until it is juxtaposed against the opposing concept of monarchy.

The word "sovereignty," or "*supremas*" in Latin, means the highest authority. The modern meaning of sovereignty was introduced late in the 16th century by the French political philosopher Jean Bodin and refers to the monarch as the sovereign. For Bodin, sovereignty is the force that supersedes citizens and subjects and is above the law. The monarch himself is acknowledged to be the supreme authority. This may seem like an invitation to tyranny and depotism, but Bodin thought that the monarch was the instrument of the highest law of all – "All power is of God" – and would be checked by the need to abide by this higher law. Subsequent years, however, saw Bodin's theory abused as despotic monarchs and governments appeared. Originally conceived as concepts that signified a "rightly ordered government," "sovereignty" and "monarchy" later became sources of political unrest – most conspicuously in the revolutions in the late 18th century to overthrow such absolute monarchy. Both the American and the French Revolutions were fought over the assertion that it is citizens and subjects, not kings, who are the highest authority, and it is thus no accident that most modern Constitutions contain ringing declarations of popular sovereignty. History has been a process of transferring sovereignty from the sovereign to the people.

By the same token, however, the concept of popular sovereignty is obviously meaningful only in light of these historical confrontations – and no such revolution occurred to confer power on the people in Japan. Generations of Japanese emperors historically called their subjects *oomitakura* or "our great treasure," and regarded the well-being and security of the people as the greatest political good and guiding precept. The concept of popular sovereignty is therefore completely irrelevant in the Japanese context. When Japan's first written Constitution was drafted in 1889, there was much contentious discussion about how to handle the principle of popular sovereignty. In the end, it was decided that the concept's premise of antagonism between ruler and ruled did not accord with – was inimical to – Japan's national polity. One might take this as evidence that the Meiji Constitution of 1889 did not accept popular sovereignty and affirmed absolutism, but such would be a serious misreading of the reality.

This then raises the question of why popular sovereignty – a doctrine that is by nature unsuited to and unnecessary for Japan – became part of the postwar Constitution. The answer is simple: Japan was defeated in World War II and occupied by the Allied Forces, to whom it ceded power in the immediate postwar period. As victors, the Americans prepared an American-style constitution, which the Japanese government was compelled to present as its own creation.

Philosopher Jean Bodin, however, offers an additional characterization of sovereignty. Sovereignty, he says, is the absolute and perpetual power of a state. National sovereignty is usually seen as distinct from popular sovereignty, but this definition shows us that they are two indivisible dimensions of sovereignty. In other words, when a country is occupied and its national sovereignty is suspended as Japan's was, both monarchy and popular sovereignty cease to exist. The supreme authority is vested in the occupying officials, and it is they and they alone who can draw up and change the nation's highest law, the Constitution. When you think about it, it is indeed ironic that the Constitution of Japan was written by an occupying force to celebrate popular sovereignty with the words: "We, the Japanese people ..." Compounding this, Article 9 paragraph 2 – Japan's renunciation of war potential – is a clear abdication of sovereignty. The guiding concepts underlying Japan's Constitution directly contradict each other. Such is the state of our Constitution.

☐■☐ The Primary Purpose Is to Rein in the Government

Hashizume Daisaburou

Hashizume Daisaburou is Professor, Tokyo Institute of Technology Graduate
School of Decision Science and Technology.
Born in 1948. Graduated from the University of Tokyo Faculty of Letters Department of Psychology and Sociology. Specializes in theoretical sociology, sociology
of religion, modern Asian studies, and modern sociology. Among his many works
are *Hajimete no Kouzou-shugi* (Introduction to Structuralism) (Kodansha), *Ningen ni
totte Hou to wa Nani ka* (What Is Law for Us as Human Beings?) (PHP), and *Gengo/
Sei/Kenryoku: Hashizume Daizaburou Shakaigaku Ronshuu* (Language, Sex, and
Power: The Sociological Writings of Hashizume Daizaburou) (Shunjuusha).

A CONSTITUTION IS a contract. It is a legal document – a law. A constitution – that document that we respect as the foundation of government and
society – is part of the rule of law.

Yet I doubt many of us are very clear exactly what "the rule of law" means.
Thus it is worth digressing a bit in this discussion of the Constitution to look
at the history and meaning of "rule of law."

Rule of law is a concept dating back to the Romans. The cornerstone of
Roman law was the idea of equality: equality without respect to pedigree or
social status – equality under the law and equality in the courts. This idea of
equality before the law was passed down to us through Judeo-Christian and
Islamic law. Today, the idea of the rule of law is accepted just as if it were a
natural law like the law of gravity.

The rule of law is easiest to understand in comparison with the "rule of God"
and the "rule of man." Monotheistic religions such as Judaism, Christianity,
and Islam believe that the world was created by God and God is supreme. God
is mankind's lord and we are his servants. Therefore, theocracy – the rule of
God – is the natural social order. God is the king.

Here we come to a difficulty in that God cannot be physically present and see to our everyday mundane needs. Because of this, the Word of God is seen as existing in a contract or covenant such as the Torah, the Bible, or the Koran, and everyone is expected to make God's rule on earth reality by obeying God's mandate as embodied in this contract or "law" and creating a social order governed by the rule of divine law. A theocratic culture thus reveres the rule of God (which becomes the rule of law) and opposes the rule of man. Monotheism believes that man must not rule man without the guidance of God. Of course, the reality is that all governments consist of people ruling other people, but the theoretical construct in a theocracy is that – authorized by God – the ruler has a "divine right" to rule.

To sum up so far, the rule of law is a way for people to avoid the overt rule of man. All human beings are free and equal. Man's rule of man would trample on these principles. God is the source of the law, and the law is fundamental.

In civilizations that were not monotheistic, however, the rule of law did not take root. In ancient China, for example, law was by imperial edict and man ruled man. Rule of law was subordinate to the rule of man and not an alternative. Rulers were not bound by law and the people disliked law, believing it inimical to their rights and liberties. Japan adopted China's legal codes, and those attitudes prevail here as well. No one wants to be subject to a ruler's whim. Opposing the rule of man, we therefore oppose the rule of law as well.

To put the Japanese attitude toward law in a nutshell, man ruling man is not a good idea. Nor is it good for laws to stand between people. The best solution is for people to live together peacefully. For this, they must be in close contact and work for common goals. The Japanese prefer to trust good will rather than rely on law.

The Japanese resist the rule of law because they resist the rule of man. Man wants freedom from rule by fellow men. But government, of course, is necessary, and this brings us back to man ruling man. As we can see in recent Japanese history, it is difficult to control government just by writing laws.

Historically, the autocratic government of the Meiji era came first, and then the Meiji Constitution of the Empire of Japan in 1889. The government existed first and wrote the Constitution out of necessity. The same holds true for the current Constitution, which was written by the American Occupation forces to suit their own purposes. Having not written the Constitution in the first place, the Japanese hesitate to try to amend (rewrite) it – which is why the Constitution has not once been amended after all these years.

Society changes and moves on, no matter how many noble sentiments are inscribed in its constitution. The disparity between today's reality and the text of Japan's Constitution grows too wide to overlook. Anyone can spot the inconsistencies; Article 9 is just the most obvious. But even then, the Constitution is not revised. In fact, there is no need to rewrite the Constitution because the government transforms it by reading new meaning into its provisions. In the most profound sense, this means that the Constitution is not a real contract between the people and their government. No document that does not restrain the government can be called a Constitution. The Japanese Constitution will lose its authority if it is left unchanged.

But time brings change. Even if the Japanese do not have a fully developed understanding of the rule of law, they must now discuss constitutional reform. It may be that they do not fully understand the rule of law because they never gave serious thought to the concept of the rule of God. Still, if Japan succeeds in constitutional revision – no matter what choices are made – it will be a job well done.

□■□ Build Compassion into the Constitution

Fujiko Hemming

Fujiko Hemming is a pianist.
Born in Berlin to Japanese mother and Russian-Swedish father. Moved to Japan
at age of three. Debuted while still a student at Aoyama Gakuin High School.
Gave up Swedish citizenship at age of 18 and became stateless. Studied at Tokyo
National University of Fine Arts and Music. Claimed refugee status and moved
to Germany at age of 29. Later lost her hearing and suffered other hardships.
Returned to Japan upon the death of her mother. Her performances have been
featured on NHK, and she has a large following.

HAVING HAD SWEDISH citizenship and having lived in Germany for many
years, I was not real sure what is in the Japanese Constitution. I did not really know what it says. But I could guess it talks about the Imperial system. I
did not even know about Article 9 and its renunciation of war. But everyone
knows you shouldn't make war, don't they? After all, war costs all kinds of
money and you don't get anything out of it in return. Some people thought
the war on Iraq was justified to get rid of Saddam Hussein, but looking at the
pictures from Abu Ghraib, I wonder how much things have really changed.
Japan should pull out of Iraq now.

When I think of Japan, I suspect things are no different from what they
were during the long centuries when the Tokugawa shogunate ruled and the
country was cut off from the rest of the world. Every time I get off the plane at
Narita, I feel like people are picking on me – even though I am a law-abiding
performing artist. This is a very narrow-minded country where the island
mentality prevails. It is outrageous.

By contrast, when I am in Europe, I have the feeling that all doors are open.
If you obey the laws and have a little money, you can live just like anyone else. I
live in Paris now, where I have many wonderful friends and am very happy.

Yet happy does not mean complacent. For example, I recently gave UNICEF ¥10 million for street-children relief. For just five times that, I could probably have bought a castle. But what would I do with a castle? Sure, I could live there with my cats, but all of the ghosts would probably come out at night and it would be creepy. I don't want to live like that. I can't do that. Hasn't it been said that those who have should give to those who have not? So I want to help the less fortunate and the disadvantaged.

When I was alone and listless in Germany, it was my cats that rescued me. I was always talking to my cats. I feel at peace when I am talking to my cats. So no matter how down and out I might be, I will always take care of my cats. The German Constitution has a provision explicitly on animal welfare.* Despite this, one of my neighbors there took me to court because of my cats. She said the fact that I have so many cats creates a sanitation and hygiene hazard. But based on the spirit of animal rights protection in the Constitution and other laws, even if the courts can order me to get rid of the rugs that smell like cat piss and to keep my home cleaner, they cannot order me to get rid of my cats. In fact, I won the court case.

In Japan too, I have a pet-sitter for my suburban Tokyo house in Shimokitazawa and provide shelter for stray cats. When I find stray cats, I pick them up, get them spayed, and try to find good homes for them. I also give about ¥2 million a year to the local merchants' association to help them help the strays. Next I plan to support the non-profit Neko no Dairinintachi (On Behalf of Cats) organization. But right now I am taking in a lot of sick cats and other cats nobody else will take in. I have a score or so, and the neighbors may be wishing I would live somewhere else.

But unlike my German neighbor, my Japanese neighbors do not sue me. This is one of the great things about Japan. If there is a major earthquake, all of the people in the community help each other. There is a tremendous spirit of mutual assistance and consideration. Germans do not need anybody's help, so they tend to be self-centered and to think just of themselves. Everybody is independent, and they go through life with a frown.

Still, I suspect Japan is 50 years behind in animal rights protection. There

---

* The German Constitution was amended in July 2002 to include Article 20a: "The State, in a spirit of responsibility for future generations, also protects the natural living conditions and the animals within the framework of the constitutional rule…" Such a clause extending animals fundamental animal rights on a par with fundamental human rights is very unusual. – Ed.

are a lot of stray cats, and a lot of cruelty to animals. I very much agree with Anatole France, who wrote that cruelty to animals is a crime against nature. Nothing is worse than cruelty to some helpless creature. Even just a single animal can provide succor for countless people. This is especially important for older people. There are some places in Japan where you are not allowed to have a cat, but this is outrageous. In Germany, people can have their pets in their hospital rooms. Anything less is a travesty. That's the kind of place I think I want to die.

But until then, I see my mission in life as being to help the disadvantaged.

(interview-based)

□■□ Include International Defense and International Citizenship

Hinohara Shigeaki

Hinohara Shigeaki is Honorary President and Director of St. Luke's International Hospital, President Emeritus of St. Luke's Nursing College.
Born in 1911, Graduated from Kyoto Imperial University Faculty of Medicine and went to work for St. Luke's International Hospital in 1941. Coined the term "shin-roujin" (new old people) to refer to active people 75 or older and started the Shin-roujin Movement to encourage people to keep trying new things as he himself does. Among his works is the mega-best-selling book *Ikikata Jouzu* (Living Smart) (U-League).

THE PREAMBLE TO the Constitution speaks of our having "determined to preserve our security and existence, trusting in the justice and faith of the peace-loving peoples of the world." Yet given that there are a number of countries that, even as they proclaim their devotion to peace, possess nuclear weapons for their national defense, the text of the Constitution – created in the immediate aftermath of the war – seems an empty letter. This is emerging as a major problem.

Likewise, the Preamble also says "we recognize that all peoples of the world have the right to live in peace, free from fear and want." But looking at the reality in Africa and elsewhere, it is clear that assistance from Japan and the other wealthy countries is essential if these people's right to live in peace free from fear and want is to mean anything. Yet in truth, it would be hard to say that Japan is very concerned about these people or that we are curtailing our own consumption and excesses in a determined effort to ensure they have a better life.

Neither before nor after the war has Japan diverted funds from its defense budget to helping the people in countries plagued by fear and want. I thus believe it would be a major contradiction for Japan to approve this Preamble as it stands without serious rethinking of its current ethnocentric policies and the dearth of concern for Africa's wellbeing.

Nor have Japanese made sufficient effort to defend their homeland – even compared to the people of those European countries commonly referred to as neutrals. For the full 60 years since the end of the war, Japan has taken the easy out and lived under U.S. military protection, the SDF being relegated to purely domestic tasks. There has been no effort to involve the people in this, and this whole approach has been very irresponsible. Little wonder young people are so apathetic about what happens to Japan.

Nor has there been much discussion and debate on whether or not Japan would be able to preserve the peace on its own. And if it turns out that Japan cannot preserve the peace on its own, Japan would have to resign itself to destruction if another country attacked. Without any popular consensus on such issues, Japan has to depend on the military backing of friendly countries such as the United States.

The international situation is now radically different from what it was when the Constitution was adopted. I think it is unrealistic to expect the rest of the world to defend Japanese sovereignty unless such issues are fully debated. While the Preamble says that "we desire to occupy an honored place in an international society striving for the preservation of peace, and the banishment of tyranny and slavery, oppression and intolerance for all time from the earth," there is a major disparity between this text and the current state of the international society. Both the government and the people should face up to the fact that the foreign policies exercised to date "to occupy an honored place" have not worked to win Japan this "honored place."

In lieu of national military conscription, I would propose a system whereby all citizens who reach the age of 20 are required to spend six months to a year somewhere working for peace or performing medical, welfare, educational, public hygiene, or other services.

More than 15 years ago, then-WHO Director-General (Dr Halfdan T.) Mahler told me that if Japan wants to play a leadership role in the international community, it should first take the initiative in offering to help those countries most in need of assistance. The idea of drawing some benefit from the countries it helps should be at most a secondary consideration. In saying this, he said he was reminded of the great Danish philosopher who said the conscious decision to give – to help someone else – is also a conscious decision to sacrifice. This was at a meeting I attended in the company of Dr Mahler and some Japanese government officials, and at the time I assumed Dr Mahler, being a Christian, was quoting Kierkegaard.

I also felt that he was tacitly criticizing Japanese foreign policy efforts, which have been based not on give and take but rather on take and give. In effect, Japan's first policy inclination has been to develop markets in the other country, to sell Japanese products there, and to reap enormous profits – this even before extending assistance.

Yet for the future, I believe it will be impossible to hope for world peace unless the haves first give to the have-nots and the talented give to the less talented. Each and every one of us should start with giving.

Today, such neutral countries as Switzerland and Sweden, as well as countries such as Germany, France, and Italy, have military conscription so that they will have the military forces they need for their self-defense, and people who refuse conscription are required to perform medical, welfare, or other public service. Educational policy and progressive initiatives by responsible government officials work to instill these principles and practical moral values in young people so that they understand what they need to do to ensure their country's defense.

I think it would be irresponsible of Japan as a state to just continue on with the current Constitution, taking the easy way out and relying upon other countries. Thus I strongly advocate the adoption of a Constitution that requires that the people be willing to defend the country and to serve overseas in less developed countries and countries that have been devastated by war or natural disaster.

☐■☐ Strengthening the Constitution to Lock Progress In

Hosokawa Morihiro

Hosokawa Morihiro is a former Prime Minister.
Born in 1938. Graduated from Sophia University Faculty of Law in 1963. Went to
work for *Asahi* newspaper upon graduation. Elected to the House of Councillors in
July 1971. Served two six-year terms. Elected Governor of Kumamoto Prefecture
in 1983. Helped found Nihon Shintou (Japan New Party) in 1992 and served as its
President. Elected to the House of Representatives in 1993 and selected as Japan's
79th Prime Minister that July. Stepped down in April 1994. Retired from the House
of Representatives and politics in 1998.

IT IS NOW more than 50 years since the Constitution was promulgated. At
first, there were times when it did not seem to fit Japan's situation. But now it
seems to be working very smoothly, even if there are a few areas such as the
use of public monies to assist private educational institutions that might once
have raised questions. While there is obviously room for thought in light of
the new rights-consciousness in line with the changes in Japan's responsibilities in the international community and the changing times, I have long
contended that, considering the political cost of rewriting the Constitution,
these are not issues that need to be addressed right away. This is also what
I had in mind when I spoke of "rewriting the Constitution stronger" when
we formed the JNP in 1992. Even the Constitution is not writ in stone, and it
would be wrong to be unthinkingly, categorically against even discussing its
amendment, and my argument was that we should be willing to amend the
Constitution if there were a clear national consensus in favor of this. Recent
public opinion polls have showed increasing support for Constitutional reform, but there is still no need to rush.

Like any other Constitution, Japan's is a product of history. If you see this
history as one of defeat, occupation, and the Americans' imposing an alien

Constitution on Japan, then you will end up in favor of the traditional arguments for a Japan-generated Constitution that are made by those who want to amend. Yet this recounting of history starts with Japan's defeat and studiously avoids mention of the wartime years.

In my first press conference after assuming the post of Prime Minister, I termed the Pacific War "a war that was wrong." The LDP immediately accused me of insulting the war dead, but I do not believe that respect for the dead can or should be used to justify the state policies that led to war or the government policies in pursuit of war.

No nation that is unable to make an honest accounting of its history is in any position to talk of contributing to the international community. The people who say they want to revise Article 9 argue that they want to include a clear provision that the Self-Defense Forces can be sent overseas not to resolve any international dispute to which Japan might be party but to contribute to the international community. Yet there is no way I can favor this if it includes allowing the use of force overseas. The current advocacy of contributing internationally is simply an adjunct to U.S. strategy now that the U.S. is no longer able to unilaterally impose its vision of world order. It is clear from events in Iraq what will inevitably come of such one-sided efforts to impose the American world order.

Prime Minister Koizumi has announced his intent to have the SDF take part in the multinational coalition based upon UN Security Council Resolution 1546, but I cannot condone the use of military force overseas by the SDF even if it is part of a UN operation. The use of military force demands of the troops that they be prepared to die if worse comes to worst. There is no justification for this other than in defense of country and family. The state cannot and should not ask any individual to die for some international contribution. Article 9 draws a clear line against the use of military force overseas, and it is a line that Japan must not cross. Can we not learn from history?

Another misgiving I have about the current effort to rewrite the Constitution is with the way its advocates see and describe the state. Some of the people who advocate rewriting the Constitution lay heavy emphasis on Japanese history and Japanese culture and promote greater "love of country." Yet the Constitution is inherently a document setting forth what the state guarantees its citizens (e.g., basic human rights) and elucidating transparently how the state will operate (the governing mechanisms). It is not a document that imposes duties and obligations on the people. When the bill to declare *Kimigayo* the national anthem and the Hinomaru flag the national flag was proposed, I argued that both have been generally accepted as such by the people but that these are not things that should be legislated and imposed by law. Japanese culture and Japanese history belong to all of the people, and it is not the Constitution's place to force this or that part on the citizenry.

Rather, what we need is a clear Constitutional definition of the state. Like Japan, Germany and Italy also rebuilt new states out of the ashes of wartime defeat, and both of their Constitutions include clear statements of the nature of the state: "a democratic and social federal state" in Germany's case and "a democratic republic based on labor" in Italy's. Neither refers to ethnicity or history. And this is as it should be in any Constitution's envisioning of the state.

If such a provision were to be added to the Japanese Constitution, it should include, for example, mention of peace, democracy, and respect for the dignity of the individual. While we often hear people argue that the current Constitution only sets forth the rights of the people, that this imbalance has led to an erosion of public-spiritedness, and that there should therefore be more emphasis on the public weal, this idea of public weal is a principle that only comes into play to reconcile the conflict of individual rights. Having the state try to impose public-spiritedness and the public good from above could well have a chilling effect on social progress and development powered by free individual creativity and vitality. The real need of the state in the 21st century is for a spirit of tolerance receptive to a diverse citizenry and vibrant culture.

To sum up, there are places where the Constitution could stand strengthening. Three that come particularly to mind are the legislative branch, especially the operation of the two Houses, the Cabinet system, and the judicial system, including the possible establishment of a Constitutional court. There are many points that should be rethought given our experience with democracy over the last 50-plus years. Yet this is no reason to favor or even allow rewriting that is secretly intended to turn back the hands of history.

□■□ Add Rights and Duties Attuned to Society's Evolution

Hotta Tsutomu

Hotta Tsutomu is a lawyer and Director of Sawayaka Welfare Foundation.
Born in 1934. Graduated from Kyoto University Faculty of Law. Led the Special
Prosecutors Team in the Lockheed bribery case in the 1970s. Retired from the Min-
istry of Justice in 1991 after serving as Director of the Ministry of Justice Minister's
Secretariat and in other posts. Founded Sawayaka Law Office and Sawayaka
Fukushi Suishin Center (now Sawayaka Welfare Foundation). Among his works are
Kabe wo Yabutte Susume (Going Through the Walls) (Nikkei Businessjin Bunko).

THE CURRENT CONSTITUTION sets forth universal principles common to all humankind, and its basic principles should be left unchanged. Yet the international community and Japanese society have both evolved significantly over the last half-century, and the Constitution needs to be amended taking account of these changes. I would make five suggestions.

On the renunciation of war (Article 9)

SUGGESTION 1: Japan should maintain the renunciation of war but allow the possession of military forces for self-defense. However, the right of collective self-defense should not be allowed, since the U.S. and U.K. interpret this more broadly than Japan does (or Germany and France do) and it would open a dangerous door.

The SDF should then be seconded to a UN force for the defense of democracy and international peace, and it should be possible to put the SDF under UN command. Since terrorism is not amenable to solution by military means, an international police force should be established soon under UN leadership and Japan should participate in all aspects of its operations to ferret out and deal with terrorists.

EXPLANATION: War between democracies is now unthinkable, and the only wars will be wars initiated by dictators, clans, or terrorists or wars preemptively initiated by democracies in order to suppress dictators, clans, or terrorists. Thus a UN force must be established to suppress acts of war and an international police structure put in place to apprehend terrorists, and Japan should be fully supportive of such UN efforts.

On the rights and duties of the people (Chapter III)

SUGGESTION 2: I would add the right to privacy within the right to freedom and add the right to know and environmental rights as social rights.

I would also add child rearing to the "marriage" section of Article 24 Paragraph 1 so that it speaks of "mutual cooperation with the equal rights of husband and wife as a basis" in child-rearing as well.

Likewise, I would add that "the right to a family name shall not be abridged by marriage" to Paragraph 2 of the same Article 24.

To Article 38 Paragraph 1 (the right to remain silent), I would add a prohibition against false testimony.

EXPLANATION: Environmental rights must be established for all posterity from a global perspective. And efforts must be made to reconcile the right to privacy and the right to know. Parental cooperation in child rearing is a critical issue for Japan. The right of husband and wife to have different family names if they wish derives from respect for the individual and equality of the sexes. The right to remain silent is massively misunderstood in Japan, with the result that criminals and defendants often engage in outright lying. It is essential to note that the right to remain silent is simply that – the right to remain silent.

On finance (Chapter VII)

SUGGESTION 3: The latter part of Article 89 (the prohibition against using public monies for charitable enterprises and the like) should be abolished, since it is a counter-productive restriction, and in its place should be the duty to support with public monies those activities that benefit the general public.

EXPLANATION: Education, welfare, and other activities traditionally conducted for the public good are seldom viable as for-profit enterprises, and the government typically assists and subsidizes them with tax monies in the public interest. Now that Japan has achieved rapid growth and the foundations of the people's economic livelihood are quite firm, the people are not content merely to have their survival guaranteed; they have come to also demand psychological elements such as welfare, respect for the individual, environmental beauty, cultural living, friendship and other comfortable interpersonal relations, and more. These new public goods differ from the traditional public goods. They are highly individualistic and diverse; they are very non-standard; they do not lend themselves to satisfaction by the government; and they are best left to volunteer public activities by citizens with a wide diversity of values. Because people pay taxes in support of public goods whether old or new, the government should have a duty to disburse tax monies as appropriate in support of these new public goods.

On local self-government (Chapter VIII)

SUGGESTION 4: Local governments should have complete legislative and executive rights over all matters pertaining to the people within their jurisdictions (including taxation). However, this provision should go into effect, under a supplemental provision, ten years after its adoption (or at such time as local governments are consolidated into "states" or some other structure, whichever comes first).

SUGGESTION 5: Local governments should be required to support citizen activities contributing to society and mutual assistance and to respect such initiatives, as well as to respect the political and social opinions of the citizenry.

EXPLANATION: The current Constitution is an effort to achieve indirect democracy with elected representatives, and it stipulates that acting in the public interest and achieving the public good are the executive branch's responsibility. Yet as the people have come to demand higher levels and greater diversity of public goods, it has become increasingly difficult for representative democracy to respond to these demands. Just as the people have taken the initiative in a wide range of public-interest activities, they have also spoken out on political and social issues, not through their representatives but directly. If local governments are to serve the people and meet their needs, it is essential they provide maximum access to information, shape policy to reflect local opinion, respect public-interest citizen initiatives, and provide these initiatives with publicity, cooperation, and other support.

□■□ Let the People Decide

Igarashi Takayoshi

Igarashi Takayoshi is Professor, Hosei University Faculty of Law, and a lawyer.
Born in 1944 in Yamagata Prefecture. Graduated from Waseda University Faculty
of Law in 1966. Specializes in urban policy, legislative studies, and public works.
Among his works are *Utsukushii Toshi wo Tsukuru Kenri* (The Right to Create Beauti-
ful Cities) (Gakugei Shuppansha), *Shimin no Kenpou* (The People's Constitution)
(Hayakawa Shobo), and the co-authored *Koukyou Jigyou wa Tomaruka* (Is There
No Stopping Public Works?) (Iwanami Shinsho).

IN ONE OF my university seminars I discussed the high-profile kidnapping
and threatened murder of three Japanese citizens in Iraq in 2004, and the
way the Japanese government castigated the three individuals and made
heavy weather of the fact that actions have consequences and that people
are responsible for these consequences. Every single student knew about the
kidnappings, but, as I expected, almost no one had discussed the situation
with friends or parents. Those who trumpet personal responsibility say that
people have to accept the consequences of doing something dangerous, and
most of my students agreed. When I asked them about the controversial dispatch of the Japanese Self-Defense Forces to Iraq, they replied that these men
and women knew what they were signing up for and could quit if they did not
want to go. My university is located near the political heart of Tokyo and was
once famous for its student protest movements. But even though my students
are political science majors, they never discuss politics. They are typical of the
whole campus, a place where politics has disappeared.

Recent (May 3, 2004) media surveys indicate that the public has become extraordinarily interested in constitutional revision and especially the right of
collective self-defense and Article 9. The polls reveal sharp fissures between
those who support revision and those who oppose it. Yet I wonder about the

results of such surveys, since they certainly do not jibe with what I get from my students. And I suspect the students are more representative of their parents and society at large than the polls are. To speculate, I further suspect people are responding facilely to survey questions because they do not perceive themselves as having a personal stake in the Constitutional reform issue.

Yet if students will look at their own lives, they will see that they and their families face the same problems that confront society at large: the issue of nursing care for an aging society, corporate layoffs in the face of recession, and dysfunctional families and rising crime rates. All of these problems impact their lives.

What is to be done? The public is divided. There are those who want to move very cautiously and hope to muddle through today's anxiety and unrest, while others want to move boldly and change government – and especially its basic law, the Constitution. The Constitution is at a crossroads. The cautious group dominates Japan today. The truth of the matter is that students are not interested in making waves. Once they have completed their coursework and graduation seems assured, they start shooting resumes out to companies. Once they have nailed down the promise of a job, they lose all interest in college. As new members of the workforce, they throw themselves into their careers, and politics is not a concern.

But, I tell them, *you* are the foundation of government. Your vote can change government policy. More than 30,000 people commit suicide every year in Japan. That's equivalent to the population of a small town. At this rate, we are losing the equivalent of a prefectural capital every ten years. It is as if a war were taking place within Japan. The European Union and our neighbors – China, Taiwan, and Korea – are all discussing constitutional reform. One of the main topics is whether the public has the right to make policy through direct democracy and national referenda. More and more nations have constitutions that give their citizens direct input into decisions. In such states, the public is the source of legitimacy and stands above legislative bodies. Since the 2004 Olympics in Athens – the birthplace of democracy – there has been a worldwide resurgence of interest in this two-thousand-year-old experiment we call democracy.

Students these days generally listen with interest when I discuss such topics. When I say something will be on the test, they take notes. When I assign something as homework, they fire up their computers, research the subject, and hand in papers. Yet they seem unable to connect what they have learned in the classroom with reality – reality such as the three Japanese hostages in

Iraq and the Japanese government's assertion of personal responsibility. The unseemly state of affairs in the Diet, which is supposed to be the sole and highest organ of state power, makes a mockery of my sermon that each and every one of them can transform politics. It is not the students' fault they do not believe me. It is the example we have set. If we are unwilling to take initiative and work for change, how can we fault the students for being apathetic and apolitical?

There have, however, been a number of instances over the last decade or so in which the public has participated vigorously in government. All over the country, people have been calling for local referenda on such topics as nuclear power stations, dams, U.S. military bases, industrial waste sites, and city mergers. Not all of these referenda have been held, as local councils are notoriously reluctant to give the people a direct say, but local groups are increasingly pushing their legislatures to institute referenda. And in some instances they have succeeded in overturning the decisions of their prefectural legislatures, governors, and even the national government. Such actions have great educational value in illustrating an essential truth for Japan: the people should make the decisions on matters that impact their lives. Personal responsibility is both wonderful and harsh – both pleasant and arduous. Referenda give us the hope and the faith that we can make a difference.

Japanese citizens can take the initiative when necessary and need not passively entrust all legislative power to the Diet. Popular sovereignty means just what it says: the people decide. This is the basic tenet of my book *Shimin no Kenpou* (The People's Constitution). Indeed, this is even more important than the arguments over revising Article 9, for it speaks the underlying truth to the public: What kind of a Constitution do you want for the 21st century?

☐■☐ The Death of Popular Sovereignty and the Rule of Law

Kaneko Masaru

Kaneko Masaru is Professor, Keio University Faculty of Economics.
Born in 1952. Completed doctoral course at University of Tokyo Graduate School.
Specializes in system economics, fiscal policy, and local government finance. Has
spoken out on a wide range of issues, including pension reform and the war in
Iraq. Is a familiar figure in print and on television. Also has many books to his
credit, among them *Funshoku Kokka* (The State's Crooked Balance Sheets) (Ku-
dansha Gendai Shinsho) and *Gyaku-shisutemugaku: Shijou to Seimei no Shikumi wo
Tokiakasu* (Reverse Systemology: Revealing the Mechanisms of Markets and Life)
(Iwanami Shinsho).

KOIZUMI JUN'ICHIROU IS about to lead us into a debate on constitutional reform, but the constitutional revisionists and preservationists don't realize that
they have fallen into the same trap.

The old revisionists had a sense of propriety. They more or less guarded the
principle of rule of law, and they accepted the Constitution as their premise
even when trying to change it. Even though they seemed to keep coming
up with one tortured reinterpretation after another, former Prime Minister
Nakasone and the other old-style revisionists respected the fundamentals
and insisted that the Constitution would have to be amended before the Self-
Defense Forces could be sent overseas.

Prime Minister Koizumi is a different matter. He dispatched an Aegis
destroyer to the Indian Ocean as backup support for the military action in
Afghanistan. He supported the Iraq War. He sent the Self-Defense Forces
to Iraq. However, he did this by manipulating the political atmosphere and
never said a word about its constitutionality. He demonstrated awesome
ignorance in citing the preamble of the Constitution to justify dispatch-
ing troops to Iraq, but it was his joining the multinational coalition in Iraq

that truly crossed the line. Bush and Koizumi are cut out of the same cloth: Koizumi made promises on his own and never personally went to the Diet and debated them. Everything took place with *ex post facto* consent.

It was said in excuse that nothing would have changed even if the Liberal Democratic and Komei ruling parties had debated this. This is government without debate, and approval is always after the fact. The man in the street may reluctantly go along and think, "The result would be the same either way. No debate? That's just the way things are." But what are the consequences? Before we knew it, participation in the multinational coalition had exceeded anything envisioned by the Constitution and the Iraq Special Measures Law. Diet debate will become meaningless if we skip Diet procedures, make unilateral decisions, and approve them after the fact. After a while we won't need a national Diet or representatives. And since democracy is inefficient, we won't need it either.

If things come to this pass, it's just the same as not having a constitution. The major premises of the Constitution – popular sovereignty, parliamentary democracy, and rule of law – are disappearing from Japan today. All we talk about is Article 9, but we should pay much more attention to the impending destruction of popular sovereignty and rule of law – the very heart of the Constitution.

Most likely, the debate over the Constitution is just getting started. Even so, the odds are high that constitutional revision won't happen in the next two years. Because of this, preservationists and others who oppose constitutional revision may mistakenly think that their claims have won the day. We have to keep a close watch, however, because Prime Minister Koizumi is the LDP's ultimate con man. In this role, he piles up one *fait accompli* upon another and radically widens the gap between reality and the Constitution. In the end, there'll be no choice but to bring the Constitution into line with the new reality.

A look at the prime minister's remarks reveals a lot about his tricks. His comments have been widely reported by the media, and each time they leave us aghast. When challenged about the basis for his assertions that Iraq had weapons of mass destruction, Koizumi retorted, "Just because we can't find President Saddam Hussein doesn't mean that Hussein doesn't exist." But, of course no such weapons were found. Asked how he can be sure the Self-Defense Forces will not be in a combat situation, Koizumi said, "You ask which are combat zones and which are non-combat zones. How should I know?" But if he cannot tell the difference, how can he say he is only sending the Self-Defense Forces to non-combat zones? Asked about his pension-plan participation, he said, "Things happen. There are all kinds of companies. There are all kinds of employees. That's life." Yes, that's true, but Koizumi is the one who violated the law when that company improperly funded his employee pension. The examples go on and on.

It's the same with economic policy. Koizumi talked about not wasting money building highways to nowhere, but meanwhile he consolidated the highway corporations, hid their bad debts, and kept on building. He continues to cut corporate taxes and give tax breaks to the rich. The national debt is now ¥703 trillion, and if we go on this way we'll never be able to pay off this massive debt. But Koizumi says he won't raise the consumption tax rate. If he completes his term, that means the consumption tax rate will stay unchanged until 2006 – at which point the baby boomers will be heading into retirement, burdening the pension system with a steep rise in disbursements. It's clear that pension financing will collapse, social security costs will balloon, and the nation's finances will be untenable. Ultimately, the only way out will be to raise taxes. Once again, we can see Koizumi up to his tricks as he changes reality and makes us adjust to it.

The wider the disparity between the reality and the Constitution, the more popular sovereignty and rule of law will crumble. It is these, and not Article 9, that are the most fundamental principles of the Constitution. We must be more cognizant of this.

Koizumi may be the prime minister who destroys Japan. The only way to stop this disaster in the making is to get rid of him. If we don't restore popular sovereignty and rule of law – the underlying concepts of the Constitution – Japan is doomed.

(interview-based)

□■□ Enhancing Tolerance of Local Government Diversity

Katayama Yoshihiro

Katayama Yoshihiro is Governor of Tottori Prefecture.
Born in 1951. Graduated from University of Tokyo Faculty of Law in 1974. Went to work for the Ministry of Home Affairs (MoHA). Served as National Tax Administration Agency Noshiro Tax Office Director, Tottori Prefecture Financial Division Director, Private Secretary to the Minister of Home Affairs, MoHA International Relations Planning Director, Tottori Prefecture General Affairs Department Director, and MoHA Prefectural Tax Division Director before retiring from the Ministry in 1998. Elected Tottori Governor in 1999 and re-elected in 2003.

CHAPTER VIII OF the Japanese Constitution is about local self-government. It states, "Regulations concerning organization and operations of local public entities shall be fixed by law in accordance with the principle of local autonomy." It has long been noted that the phrase "the principle of local autonomy" lacks specificity and needs clarification with legislation elucidating the principles of local autonomy. Local government must operate in ways that reflect the will of the people, and legislation should not lock in unrepresentativeness. There is thus great significance to expressing and reaffirming these principles within the Constitution.

The Constitution secures democracy and provides for reflecting the will of the people by means of direct public elections to select the officials and assembly members who will represent the people. But what is the reality of local government conducted with representatives chosen this way? From the public's point of view, how many local governments actually do a good job of staying in step with and representing the people? Unfortunately, not very many.

One reason for this disparity is that assembly members are not representative of the public spectrum. More than half of the working population are office workers, and these are the citizens who pay the largest share of local income taxes. But almost none of the legislators who represent them are currently employed as ordinary office workers. Local governments typically deal with the everyday problems that members of the public face, such as child rearing and education. The reality of public life, however, is that any individual who wants to take part in local government and work to resolve these problems must usually give up his life as an everyday wage earner and become a professional politician. Only very extraordinary people are willing to do this.

Which brings us to the second reason for this gap between the popular will and local government: even with a functioning electoral system, the number of people who are willing to serve as local government officials or representatives is declining precipitously. In many small towns and villages, local candidates run unopposed. An uncontested election may be fine if the winner is everything he should be, but that is not always the case. Assembly elections often just barely have as many candidates as there are seats to fill. Thus the principles of healthy competition do not work and human resources quality control falls down.

Everyone wants the best for the area where he lives. But when it comes to running for election, people hang back, even if they have the ability and the aptitude for public office. Running for election means appealing to the public and convincing people you are so much more wonderful and capable than your opponent. This is not something that anyone with a sense of decorum will enjoy. And the psychological barriers to making such an appeal are especially high in areas where everyone knows everyone else.

As a result, I am in favor of letting localities with too few candidates choose a non-electoral means – such as a lottery or a rotation-based system – of selecting assembly members. In ancient Greece, Aristotle thought a rotation system was the most democratic means for selecting representatives, and a lottery the second most democratic. Aristotle held that elections choose the superior person and this weakens the identification between the rulers (the superior people who are elected) and the ruled (who elect them). He also stated that this is not necessarily democratic and is akin to an aristocracy.

Happily, Japan has a working model of an assembly of representatives chosen by lottery. This is the Hino County Council in Tottori Prefecture. Hino County now has the oldest residents and is the most depopulated county in Tottori, which is why the prefecture enacted this unique ordinance. Thirty people – young and old, men and women – are chosen by lottery to serve on the very active county council, monitoring governmental operations, making suggestions, and so on. The council members do not run for election and so do not have to engage in that eerie politician-like playing to public opinion. Instead, they engage in frank and honest discussions. I like the idea of flexible alternatives, such as letting small local governments decide to change their assemblies into such bodies. Another variation might be a bicameral assembly consisting of one chamber of "professional politicians" and a second chamber of legislators selected by lottery, each chamber about the same size. The important thing here is to be flexible.

It would also be entirely appropriate to use a non-election selection method when too few people want to be the mayor of a town or village. For example, it would not be amiss to have a quasi-parliamentary system in which the assembly members choose the mayor from among their numbers. Or perhaps they could recruit an outsider with the requisite competence and integrity to serve as municipal administrator for a fixed term supervised by the assembly.

Whatever the details, more variety is welcome, whether it is in local government administration, local assemblies, or executive offices. If we choose a system that fits the situation, we will be able to come up with local governments that are more representative of the people they serve. It is variety itself that provides the zest of local government. Of course, bringing these ideas to fruition may mean we have to revise Article 93's stipulation that officials and legislators be elected by direct popular vote. But thinking about the best way to structure local governments is a good way to get people thinking about the Constitution in real-life terms.

☐■☐ Seeing Unseen Faces, Hearing Unheard Voices

Katou Tokiko

Katou Tokiko is a singer.

Born in 1943. Graduated from University of Tokyo Faculty of Letters Department of Western History. Debuted while still a student and has performed profession-ally ever since. Has many hit songs to her credit, including "Hitorine no Komoriuta" (Lullaby for a Child Sleeping Alone), "Shiretoko Ryojou" (Sad Visit to Shiretoko), "Kono Sora wo Tobetara" (If I Could Fly), and "Hyakumanbon no Bara" (A Million Roses). Among her books are *Katou Tokiko no Otoko Moyou* (Katou Tokiko Interviews Leading Men) (Sanseido) and *Aoi Tsuki no Balaado* (Pale Moon Ballad) (Shougakkan).

I FIND MYSELF saying forlornly, "It's terrifying to grow old."

It's not just me: it's words, the world around me, ideas, serious discussions... everything.

Is it possible for things to keep the same luster and meaning from birth through to their inevitable old age? I worry.

What makes life grow stale?

Sometimes I think it is the immense power words have that spells their doom.

Those who are powerless use words and ideals to proclaim truth and hope, but those who are powerful use them to lead down an opposite path.

War in the name of *peace. Aggression* in the name of *freedom.* One after an-other, words are slain as the age seems to condone such perversion.

The difficulty today is in finding vibrant living words that ring out their meaning.

Peace and *freedom* are not the only words that are dead. There are also *de-mocracy, equality, human rights...*

Have any of the 20th-century ideals in Japan's Constitution retained their original meaning and force? To my mind, it depends on who uses these brave words and ideas.

The public must use fresh new language if the government is to be taken back from the powerful vested interests.

When we say *democracy*, the very word must elicit the face of the people; *equality* must make us see those whom it has protected and saved.

But the people's faces have vanished; their voices are unheard. Japan's future is at risk.

At its birth, the Constitution was our lodestar. One and all – teachers, policemen, students, mothers, and fathers – saw it as their guide for living.

But now, the Constitution is lost in the abyss of the Diet.

People have lost the sense that the Constitution is serving them. Despite the lofty ideals in the Constitution's Preamble, *popular sovereignty* is now just an empty phrase. What caused the people's faces to vanish; what preempted their voices?

Before the war, it was the Constitution of the Empire of Japan with its outspoken police powers over a subordinate public.

Now, I think the bloated media are minimizing the people's role.

Television, for example. People sit in front of the TV to laugh, get angry, get excited, and talk back. In no time at all, their voices and ability to communicate have disappeared into the void.

On television life is nothing more than a series of swiftly passing snapshots. Immersed in each scene, the viewer forgets how to use his own voice.

The people's voice is too low, and turning up the sound will take years.

Commentators appearing on talk shows seem to be stating their opinions, but it is only the canned controversy of TV. The host rounds off each discussion with "We will be back after this message," and each tilt at meaning ends in twelve minutes.

"Was the information correct?" you say. The answer is, "Who knows? It went over well." This is an age in which elections are fought with 60-second ads.

Those diminished individuals in front of their television sets look so small. Stand up! Say what you think! Show who you are! Reclaim your voice!

"Sovereignty resides in the people," the Constitution promises. But the national anthem starts off with the words "His Majesty's reign."

From elementary school on, we were told to sing the anthem: *Kimigayo*. If children are raised without a sense of their personal sovereignty, the Japanese Constitution will be eternally closed away behind thick doors.

This is intolerable.

This is truly an ominous era – a foreboding era – in which words keep being perverted and dying. Now more than ever, it is time to raise your voices and throw yourself into action! This is the heart and soul of Japan's peace Constitution.

◻◼◻ The Crucial Importance of Accountability
Kawada Ryuuhei

Kawada Ryuuhei is Adjunct Lecturer, Matsumoto University.
Born in 1976. Diagnosed with hemophilia at the age of six months and contracted
HIV from the transfusions received as part of his treatment. In 1993, joined the class
action suit mounted by people who had contracted HIV from blood transfusions.
Abandoned anonymity and went public in 1995. Suit was settled with a de facto vic-
tory for the plaintiffs in 1996. Took a leave of absence from Tokyo Keizai University
to go to Germany. Mother is former House of Representatives member Kawada
Etsuko. Assumed his present post in 2003. Teaches courses in social activism.

THE CONSTITUTION IS an invaluable treasure for each and every person. I
felt this particularly during our long suit over HIV-tainted transfusions. Not
only did the trial itself seem to drag on and on, we were not at all sure we
would win. My father was strongly opposed to my joining the class action.
He thought I should forget about the trial and spend my remaining years
doing things I enjoyed. Personally, I would have preferred not to think about
being ill. Having no idea how much longer I would live, I was dispirited and
wondered what the point of the trial was. But my mother said we had to take
it to court to get the truth out – that we had a duty to do this. Even though I
sometimes wondered what the point was, my mother was determined to see
this through – even to the point of getting a divorce when my father opposed
my joining the suit.

About the same time as this was going on, my high school civics class studied the legal system, and I developed a budding interest in the judiciary. I was
especially impressed by the suit Asahi Shigeru brought against the government in 1957 in an effort to get it to respect the Constitution's guarantee that
all people have "the right to maintain the minimum standards of wholesome
and cultured living." This was a case that showed me it is possible to use the

courts to transform society, even if you lose. And as I read more about the HIV-tainted blood products, I came increasingly to feel that the government and the pharmaceutical companies had acted unforgivably. I came to want to go through with this suit, if only to find out why I had been infected. The ideals that sustained me in this struggle were the right to life and the pursuit of happiness as inscribed in the Constitution.

So when I was in the 11th grade, I decided to join the class action. This case took seven long years from the initial filing until settlement. We were at an automatic disadvantage, and had it not been for the Constitution, it would have been impossible for us to take the government to court and to fight this very long battle. The more I read the Constitution, the more I was encouraged that our cause was just. This taught me how very precious the Constitution is.

A provisional judgment was handed down in the spring of 1995; we offered an out-of-court settlement in the summer, and by fall we had a groundbreaking court-initiated framework for a settlement. And then the negotiations began. I felt very keenly at the time that even though we had won the substance, the ideals and the spirit of the Constitution were still not being fully respected. In the starkest of terms, for example, the "sincere apology" that we had consistently sought was not included in the final settlement contract. If the defendants had admitted that they were in the wrong, said they were sincerely sorry, and sworn never to do something like this again, we could have accepted that as a sincere apology. But all we got was a perfunctory "sorry" – which seems to me indicative of the fact that they did not see us as real, living, breathing people. Until then, the best anyone had gotten was that the incident was "regrettable," so getting to "sorry" was progress of sorts. But when I saw this same pro forma "sorry" being trotted out to fob off the plaintiffs in the leprosy patients' class action against the government, I realized that we had failed to win the sincere apology we wanted. Even though this was a landmark case in that we won a ruling that the defendants' action was unconstitutional, the Constitution is still not fully functional and fully respected. There is still not 100% respect for the fundamental human rights enshrined in the Constitution.

This lack of respect is evident not only in our and the leprosy patients' cases. There are also reams of truly deplorable school rules and regulations that make a mockery of children's rights. Women and non-Japanese find their rights routinely infringed. The fact that the Japanese reality does not accord with the provisions of the Constitution is because we have yet to make the Constitution part of our daily lives.

There is talk of amending the Constitution, but such talk worries me. The momentum is building for change, but there are as yet few if any details on what actual changes will be sought. Instead of going along willy-nilly with the flow and talking about amending or not amending the Constitution, the important thing now is to make a concerted effort to live up to the Constitution we have. And within that, it is particularly important that Ministers of State, members of the Diet, judges, and other public officials reaffirm in their own hearts their solemn obligation to respect and uphold the Constitution as stipulated in Article 99.

At the same time, even though Article 9 is a focus of debate, Article 9 should be left as it is. The argument that Article 9 should be rewritten because it is not attuned to the current international climate is singularly unpersuasive. Rather than rewriting Article 9, we should concentrate on working all the harder to bring the international situation more into line with Article 9's ideals. Article 9 is symbolic of how forward-looking the Constitution is. Indeed, Article 9 is a statement of what all humanity must ultimately achieve – a beacon lighting the way ahead. Other constitutions not having anything even remotely similar, Article 9 is the heart and soul of the Japanese Constitution's identity. It is the one point the Japanese people most strongly advocate and take the most pride in. It would be the height of folly to dismantle Article 9 and make ours an ordinary constitution like any other.

I love Japan. But at the same time, I see Japan – a country that long refused to admit its own responsibility in the HIV-tainted blood scandal – as an adversary to be fought. The state that we saw from our perspective in that class-action suit was in no way worthy of our respect and invited only disgust and disillusionment. That is why I very much believe we need to uphold the Constitution as a brake on the blind ambitions of political leaders and state organs.

Now is not the time to amend the Constitution. Now is the time to exercise ingenuity and energy in bringing the Constitution to life and living it to the fullest.

(interview-based)

□■□ Guaranteeing Economic Rights

Kawamoto Yuuko

Kawamoto Yuuko is Professor, Waseda University Graduate School.
Graduated from University of Tokyo Faculty of Letters Department of Social Psychology. Completed graduate course in economics at Oxford University. Worked for Bank of Tokyo and then the Tokyo office of McKinsey and Company. Has served as advisor to the Financial Services Agency, on the Committee for the Privatization of the Four Highway-related Public Corporations, and in other posts. Assumed current position in April 2004. Best known for *Nihon wo Kaeru: Jiritsu shita Min wo Mezasite* (Changing Japan: For an Independent Private Sector to Transform Japan) (Chuuou Kouron Shinsha).

RECENT POLLS SHOW over half of the populace in favor of amending the Constitution, and there is increasing momentum for Constitutional reform. While most of the attention is focused on Article 9, it is important that any discussion of amending the Constitution look not just at Article 9 but at all aspects. I would thus like to address the relationship between economic policy and the Constitution.

Seen from an economic perspective, the Constitution plays a significant role in guaranteeing property rights, the freedom to run a business, and the freedom of occupational choice; in curtailing the government and limiting government intervention; and in promoting free and unfettered business activity by individuals and corporations. In that sense, the current Constitution seems to guarantee the basic framework of the Japanese economy as a market-based economy. The problem lies in the way these Constitutional provisions have been interpreted.

The traditional interpretation of the Constitution has been to impose a double standard in which the criteria and standards for allowing restrictions on economic freedoms seem to be laxer than those for allowing restrictions on freedoms of conscience, and a "rational basis" is the grounds for judgment. Likewise, the traditional interpretation is to condone government intervention in the economy when it is justified by the right to minimum standards of living as provided for in Paragraph 1 of Article 25.

But from the perspective of actual applications to real-life situations, the Supreme Court has ruled that the government may not intervene with intent to restrict economic freedoms. Should the government wish to curtail an individual's economic freedom, it must show cause why it wants to do this and must explain itself clearly with reference to the relevant laws and regulations. Even if an empowering law has been passed by the Diet, the courts will rule in favor of the individual based upon the Constitution and will invalidate the government's curtailment unless it has a reasonable basis. Similarly, the Supreme Court has found that the popular rights based upon Paragraph 1 of Article 25 are not specific tangibles but are things that should be specified by law, and in that sense has placed limits on the government's curtailment of these rights.

As a result, the current Constitution has been interpreted and enforced without any major problems. Even though it still contains the double standard in interpretation, it is very much in tune with the times. While I strongly agree that we should be most careful about imposing restrictions on freedom of expression and other freedoms of conscience and that such restrictions should be rare exceptions, at the same time I am very uncomfortable with the idea that restrictions may be placed on economic freedoms. Respect for economic freedoms is no less important to the character of the state than respect for conscience freedoms is.

The thinking behind economic policy is also changing. Given the impasse in welfare-state policies and the historical development represented by the collapse of socialism, it is increasingly understood that Japan cannot grow unless the government avoids excessive intervention and works to give full rein to the power of market economics. Any effort to amend the Constitution should take all due account of this economic reality.

In addition, it should also be possible to amend the Constitution to provide for public oversight and to build in corrective mechanisms so as to ensure that government actions do not distort the economy or place an excessive burden on it. One important element here is to have complete information disclosure on all government activities. For example, information is now available on the General Budget but not on the details of the government's Fiscal Investment and Loan Program (FILP). A considerable portion of the funds that the people have entrusted to the postal savings or pension systems is invested with an array of government organizations, and the cumulative total of all FILP funding currently runs to ¥400 trillion – an amount equivalent to the total lending by all private-sector financial institutions.

As was spotlighted in the discussions on how best to privatize the Japan Highway Public Corporation, these funds are funneled through the government and end up being invested by the public corporations. Yet some of these projects are of less-than-investment grade, and it is not always clear whether the money will ever be repaid. Because the public corporations are government bodies, it is assumed they will never default, and there are no provisions made for such a contingency. Yet because their operations are backed by the full faith and credit of the government, they are exempt from market oversight – which in turn inevitably leads to a weakening of governance mechanisms in the management of such public corporation projects. In ordinary corporate terms, it is as if the company were bleeding red ink every year but there were no rules or incentives – or even any means – for calling management to account. Even though the legal trappings have recently been tweaked to convert many of these public corporations to "independent agencies," this does not really solve the essential problem, and there is a very great danger that the recycling of public monies may ultimately end up imposing a massive burden on the people. This is much too important an issue to be left to a handful of government bureaucrats and outside experts, and I wonder if it is not the role of the Constitution to ensure enough information is readily available that the people can take a fully informed part in formulating sound fiscal policies.

I believe the government should make a proactive effort to make all of the information available on all of the government activities that the people end up paying for. The current Constitution's stipulation that the Cabinet report at least annually to the people on the state of national finances is entirely inadequate. We need a provision mandating that reports be made to the people and that all of the information be opened to public scrutiny on all government activities that might create a burden on the people. While I am not a legal expert and thus do not have definitive views about how the Constitution should be worded, the important thing is that the people, as taxpayers, have the right to demand the information they need to understand both the broader picture and the specific details.

☐■☐ The Constitution as a Statement of Identity

Kishi Beniko

Kishi Beniko is a beauty sommelier and President of Colon Inc.
Born in 1974. Graduated from Keio University. Modeled for magazines while still a student. Writes widely on and in the beauty industry, including consulting for cosmetics companies. Following graduation, created Japan's first independent website evaluating and recommending cosmetics < www.biena.net > and went into cosmetics marketing. Has lectured and written extensively on the power of beauty.

FOR THE LAST decade or so, I have been engaged in beauty marketing, have written a lot as a beauty journalist, and have been constantly preoccupied with the question of what beauty is and how it can be defined and expressed.

Looking at the Constitution from this perspective, I find the Preamble somewhat difficult and lacking in elegance. Nor do I think it contains a clear statement of Japanese values, thinking, or beliefs. It lacks personality.

Japan has a wonderful cultural heritage. Such traditional aesthetic values as *wabi* and *sabi*, for example, are uniquely Japanese and part of the Japanese identity. Even in something as seemingly simple as cosmetics, Japanese technology is outstanding. Not only product quality but also the fragrances, the shape of the containers, and everything else is done with exquisite attention to detail. Given their high added value, Japanese cosmetics are setting global standards of excellence. And Japanese women, using these cosmetics expertly, are now considered among the most beautiful in the world – women who have a superbly developed sense of beauty. Both Japan itself and its people have tremendous added value.

I think the Constitution would be vastly improved and much more attractive if this beautiful Japanese personality and pride could be incorporated in the Preamble. And would it not be so much better – so inspiring – if this were couched in beautiful language befitting this beautiful country?

I did not pay much attention to Japanese culture and the Japanese tradition of beauty when I was young. It was only when I started living and studying abroad that I noticed these things. The more the world globalizes, the more people need a firm identity they can call their own. Who am I? When I started asking myself this vexing question, I came up against the existence of Japanese culture.

Surely I am not the only one. And surely the same applies as well to a state. Japan is a country that designates and honors living national treasures and intangible cultural properties in traditional culture, crafts, and more. Seeking explicit statement of its own national identity, why should not Japan include this distinctive respect for traditional beauty in its Constitution?

There is one other facet that I would like to have included in the Constitution: the value of community and harmony. Just as a vast multitude of gods exist together in the Japanese pantheon, Japan has long had a tradition of tolerating great diversity of values. Japan has embraced a diversity of cultural traditions from overseas and has been able to Japanize them adroitly. Rather than flat-out rejecting all things foreign, Japan has brought Japanese interpretations to them, internalized them, and transformed them into Japanese originals. I would like to see this philosophy of harmonious community included in the Constitution as an evocation of this Japanese sense of beauty.

Why do I make such a proposal? Because even though the Constitution is important to you and me, we still cannot feel a real affinity for it. Very honestly, I had never before sat down and read the Constitution all the way through. I learned the basics in social science class, but that was about it. So I never really thought about it and never really saw it as forming the fundamental legal framework for the state.

Moreover, it would be safe to say that my generation – the children of the baby-boomers – and younger generations have been raised in a climate of resignation and despair. We know neither the rapid growth of the 1960s nor the bubble economy of the late 1980s. We know only the long Heisei recession of the last dozen years, when our fathers were laid off and new graduates faced a very bleak job market. Ours is a generation that has no experience with the kinds of success stories earlier generations generally took for granted. As typified by the characterizations of this generation as an untethered generation and a generation fighting just to survive, ours is a generation that has no spiritual anchorage in society and no sense of mission.

We are doing all we can simply to survive, and we never expected to get anything much from the state or politics. We do not really care about politics. Instead, we are interested in what is happening in our own lives and those of the people close to us. This is about as far as our quest for happiness extends. Like it or not, we have been forced to look for happiness within a very narrow range of options, within a small group of people. So young people such as myself are not much interested in the Constitution. Conversely, of course, knowing we cannot depend upon society or some big company, many people of my generation have succeeded in developing the personal strength they need to live on their own wits. Before these people will feel any affinity with the Constitution, it is essential the Constitution be structured to let people realize their potential and be proud to be Japanese.

Given that the Constitution is over half a century old, it is only natural there should be some places that are out of synch with our current reality. That is why it has to be rewritten in beautiful language as befits our beautiful country and has to exhibit a distinctive personality that today's young people can identify with.

For someone such as myself in constant pursuit of beauty, peace and welfare are the ultimate beauty. Which is why I feel it so important that these values embodied in the current Constitution not be tampered with.

(interview-based)

☐ ■ ☐ All Great Constitutions Are
Imposed on Governments

C. Douglas Lummis

C. Douglas Lummis is an international political scientist and Adjunct Lecturer at
Okinawa International University.
Born In 1936 in San Francisco. Studied history of political thought at the University
of California. Joined the Marines in 1960 and was sent to Japan. Currently lives
in Okinawa. Among his works are *Radical Democracy* (Cornell University Press),
Kenpou to Sensou (War and the Constitution) (Shoubunsha), and *Nihon wa Hontou
ni Heiwa Kenpou wo Suteru no desuka* (Will Japan Really Jettison Its Peace Constitution?) (Heibonsha).

I FIND IT very curious that people talk of the Constitution as having been
forced on Japan and seem to assume this is some fatal flaw. Ever since the
Magna Carta was forced on King John in 1215, all great constitutions have
been forced-on Constitutions. People who do not understand this do
not – cannot – understand what a Constitution is.

A Constitution may read like a list of rules, but the adoption of the Constitution is a very significant event in the country's political history and represents
a major exercise of power. Or perhaps it might be more accurate to say that
the Constitution is established to codify and institutionalize the gains won
by the exercise of power. The common objective of all great Constitutions is
to constrain state authority and to bend the state to the principle of rule of
law. Since the people in power have historically never moved to voluntarily
curtail their own authority, state authority can only be constrained by forcing
restraints on it.

So it is only natural that the Japanese Constitution should have been forced
on the government. Yet such is not to say that America forced this Constitu-

tion on Japan. Rather, for a short period, the American Occupation forces and the Japanese people were working for the same ends and forced the Constitution on the Japanese government. Even though they may have been working from different premises, both thought the government had grown too powerful and needed to be brought to heel.

Yet this alliance, if you will, between the Occupation forces and the Japanese people was short-lived, and there was only a very short window of opportunity in Japanese history when such a special Constitution could have been created. Once the Cold War started, the Occupation forces did an about-face in what has been called the "reverse course." Under this new course, they wanted to make Japan a strong country in the fight against Communism and started pressing Japan to revert to being a military power. And it was in this context that Japan was saddled with the Self-Defense Forces, the Security Treaty, the U.S. military bases, the arms race, the U.S.-Japan Defense Guidelines, and more. The power structure changed and the alliance shifted to one between the American government and the Japanese government to force all of these things on the Japanese people. But it has not yet been able to convert Japan into a military power able to conduct military operations and fight wars – which is surprising, considering the strength of that power alliance. The Japanese peace movement is amazingly resilient.

Of course the government politicians who hold the levers of power in Japan think this Constitution was forced on them, because this is a Constitution that sharply limits their power. And this rigor is a defining characteristic of the Constitution. As stated earlier, when the Constitution was written and adopted, both the U.S. Occupation forces and the Japanese people thought the government was too powerful and needed to be reined in. As a result, the Constitution is a major force for taking power away from the state and curtailing government authority.

The Japanese Constitution is founded on the principle that sovereignty lies with the people. As such, it marks a radical departure from the old Meiji Constitution, where everything was written in the Imperial "we" and the text was granted by the Emperor to his subjects. The current Constitution is written from a "we, the Japanese people" perspective, and the text is a series of directives from the people to the government. The people grant the government certain powers and authority, but the Constitution is very clear about exactly what powers and authority this is. Articles 1 through 40 are primarily a long list of powers and authority NOT ceded to the government (the exception being Article 30, which imposes on the people an obligation to pay taxes).

Articles 1 through 8 limit the Emperor's authority. And the articles spelling out fundamental human rights are basically telling the government what it may not do (e.g., may not limit freedom of speech, may not punish anyone without going through the judicial process, may not torture people, and may not engage in religious activity). It is not until we get to Article 41 that we finally have some provisions laying out what the government may do.

Article 9 is also in this vein, in that it is an explicit statement that the people do not grant the government the right of belligerency. This right of belligerency is often misunderstood, but it is used here in the sense of a special right accruing to the state and saying the state will not be charged with murder for killing people on the battlefield. Strictly speaking, since the state is an abstract and does not, as an abstract, have the ability to kill someone, the right of belligerency means that a soldier who kills someone on behalf of the state is not charged with murder but is treated as a hero.

It is important we be clear about this. Article 9 does not say, "The government should try to avoid wars" or "It would be nice to work for peace when possible." Article 9 is not advice, an idea, or a dream. It is an actual law that is binding on the government. The Constitution is a very clear statement of which powers the government has and which it does not have. And because powers and authority cannot be acquired other than in the Constitution (see Article 98), the fact that a power is not explicitly granted in the Constitution means the government does not have that power.

Article 12 is another interesting article. It says, "The freedoms and rights guaranteed to the people by this Constitution shall be maintained by the constant endeavor of the people." Perhaps this and Article 97 may be what is meant when it is claimed that Constitution was forced on Japan, for this is warning that the people will lose their freedoms and rights unless they constantly endeavor to maintain them, which means constant political movements, which means the people must constantly work to impose their will on the government. And the truth of this is borne out by current government trends. There is a very real danger that the Constitution – the people – might not be relentless enough in imposing the popular will on the government.

□■□ Getting Involved to Make It Happen

Mighty Crown

Based in Yokohama. Formed in 1991, this reggae group has performed all over the world, including North America, the Caribbean islands, and Europe. The core members are the two brothers main mc Masta Simon and main selector/mc Sami-T, selector/mc Super G, and selector Cojie. Over the years, Mighty Crown has produced many CDs, DVDs, live events, concerts, and even their own Life Style Records record label. Their Yokohama Reggae Festival drew 20,000+ people in the summers of 2004 and 2005. They have a strong following worldwide.

HAVING BEEN ASKED to write a short essay for this book on our thoughts on the Japanese Constitution, the four of us had an extensive discussion about it. Within our group, Simon and Sami attended an international school while Super G and Cojie attended Japanese schools. Simon and Sami were never taught about the Constitution; Super G and Cojie may have had a question or two about Article 9 on an exam, but they were not taught about the Constitution in detail. So all of us decided to read the Constitution and some of the literature on it. But in all honesty, there are a lot of things we still do not really understand about the Constitution. However, not limiting ourselves to the Constitution, we think about what is happening and what things are like in Japan and worldwide and try to incorporate our understanding in our shows, events, and recordings.

The kind of reggae music we do lends itself to powerful messages about problems in Japan and worldwide. And the style we perform in – including the whole sound system with its mobile speakers – is especially good for allowing the mc to explain the thinking behind the songs that the selector plays and to get feedback from the audience in the call-and-response format. Sometimes the selector will play a tune that the audience really likes and the venue swells with a sense of unity. Sometimes there is less resonance. The audience response differs depending upon what tune is selected and how the mc talks to the people. For instance, we may include issues such as the war in Iraq, pension funding problems, or police corruption and voice our opinions to the audience at our shows and concerts. If the audience identifies with the mc's patter on the issue, the response is stronger, if they don't, it is weaker. We don't assume that young people don't understand these things. There are young people in our audiences with great dreams and aspirations – such as dreaming of becoming a surgeon, politician, or government official. And we feel great if we can help boost their self-esteem.

In Japan as elsewhere, there are many young people who feel there is something wrong or there are problems with the way the country is being run. An example would be the Japanese pension fund problem. But as with so many other problems that the politicians and bureaucrats create, it is assumed young people cannot be trusted to understand them or even to be interested. True, it does seem at first glance as though young people are not interested in these problems. But when we speak out with a tune concerning this or that problem at an event, the audience responds and there is an obvious meeting of minds, which means that the young people do care about these political problems.

Actually, the politicians themselves are at least partly to blame for the fact that young people are assumed to be apathetic about politics and government policy. Many politicians think that young people don't know or don't understand politics. But the young people want explanations they can understand and want the politicians to walk the walk. For instance, why do we need the pension fund? For example, don't just say that graffiti is illegal but designate places where graffiti is allowed freely – don't just ban skateboarding but have parks where skateboarding is allowed. Doing small things like these for starters would really change the way young people look at politics.

On the other hand, this doesn't mean that the young people are entirely blameless. We recently saw a television talk show about war and felt that the young people's comments were unconvincing and seemed unreal. But just being young doesn't mean you are unpersuasive. There was a 21-year old member of the Self-Defense Forces on this program who would be on the front lines if Japan ever went to war, and his comments carried real weight. He was able to speak the way he did because he had a very personal stake and was always thinking about these issues. Young people shouldn't just complain about problems or issues but should put themselves in the other person's shoes and understand both sides, which will help them understand issues and solve problems better.

As a group, we try not to judge based only on one information source or rumor. For instance, even though someone might be thought of as an unsavory character, it is hard to judge the reality until you actually meet the person for yourself. It is very important not to be misled by just one source but to see things from various angles. That makes a big difference.

Politicians need to bond with the people more. We value the fact that we always bond with our audiences and that we gain a sense of unity and grow, which is why the audience response is so important. But there is no sense of unity in politics today. This is why the people do not provide any feedback. If the politicians want the people to show more interest in politics, they need to find some way for politicians and people to feel a sense of community. We hope for politicians to lead Japan and better the country. Just as we use our music to receive power from and to give power to many and various people, if the Japanese politicians are really thinking of the people, they had better think harder.

This is the Mighty Crown style. Power of one.

(interview-based)

☐■☐ Fearing for Article 9, Fearing for Japan

Miki Mutsuko

Miki Mutsuko is Takeo Miki Memorial Hall Curator, UN Women's Society Chair, and Asian Peace and Friendship Fund for Women Chair.
Born in 1917. Father was Showa Denko founder Mori Nobuteru. Married Miki Takeo at the age of 22 – when he was a first-term Diet member. Supported her husband's political career ever since and was nicknamed "Madame Prime Minister" when he was Prime Minister. Still working for Japan-China friendship and for Korean unification from a woman's perspective. Among her works is *Kokoro ni Nokoru Hitobito* (Memorable People) (Iwanami Shoten).

THE CONSTITUTION OF Japan is a peace constitution that we can be proud of before all the world. It may well be a Constitution that was forced on us by the United States in the tumultuous occupation years. There may well be places where the language is less than elegant Japanese. But if it is a good Constitution that bears repeated reading, I think we should stop fretting about its origins and treasure it.

Especially Article 9 – which is the most important part of the Constitution – should be retained. Thanks to this Constitution, Japan has been able to tell the entire world, straight-out and guilt-free, that we will not take part in any of its wars. There is no need whatever to tinker with Article 9. Yet even so, there are increasing calls to amend the Constitution, and I am worried.

Nothing else is as cruel and frightening as war. I still vividly recall the bombings during World War II. And every time I recall the U.S. bombers on their bombing runs, even today, I am seized with a paralyzing fear. I never want to experience such a frightening thing again. It is imperative that Japan not wage war.

My late husband (Miki Takeo, 1907–1988) was also adamant in his opposition to war. Miki debuted in politics at a candidates' debate held at Hibiya

Hall in February 1938. Looking at photographs of the event, I notice that the great humanist Kikuchi Kan was also on the stage. The hall was filled to overflowing, and the first words Miki spoke to the multitude were, "Japan and the U.S. should not go to war." All the more did Miki cherish the Constitution and Article 9.

I remember asking him at one point why he was in the Liberal Democratic Party, since he opposed so many of the things it stood for, and I also remember his answer: "If I left, the party would quickly move to try to amend the Constitution. So I stay in to try to deter such moves." I feel his reply was very much on the mark. No sooner had Miki died than the LDP started beating the drum for amending the Constitution.

One of the things that worries me is that Prime Minister Koizumi, Abe Shinzou, and their ilk are too young to have had any personal experience with the horrors of war. Listening to them talk, I wonder if they really understand the horror and tragedy that war inevitably brings.

Abe's grandfather on his father's side was Abe Hiroshi, who was also a Diet member. Yet like Miki, this Abe was staunchly anti-war. Even though he was pursued by the Home Ministry's dreaded Special Higher Police before and during the war, he joined Miki in traveling all over the country and speaking out against the war. Abe Shinzou is a fierce advocate of rewriting Article 9, but I wish I could have a chance to tell him some of what his grandfather said.

The people who want to rewrite Article 9 are people who want to go to war. Yet if they are so anxious to send Japanese young people off to battle that they would amend the Constitution to make this possible, why don't they first go to battle themselves? There is no need for them to put other people at risk.

At the same time as increasing calls are heard to amend the Constitution, there are also, I fear, increasing efforts being made to curtail the people's freedom of conscience. This shows up, for example, in the issue of the flag. Of course, there is nothing wrong with Japan's having a national flag. Yet the situation in Tokyo, where numerous teachers have been disciplined for failing to stand when the flag is presented, is clearly beyond the pale. I wonder if the members of the Tokyo Metropolitan Board of Education who mete out such punishment have flags at home and fly them on national holidays. Rather than go through rhetorical contortions to punish these teachers for displays of conscience, why don't they set an example by flying the flag themselves?

Nor can I muster much respect for the Japanese leaders who seem to have sold their souls to the United States. America is, you will recall, the country that dropped nuclear weapons on both Hiroshima and Nagasaki, yet no U.S.

President has visited either city. If we are going to speak of Japan-U.S. friendship, the U.S. leaders should first visit Hiroshima and Nagasaki and apologize to the *hibakusha* [atomic bomb survivors] and their families. Given this record, I find it impossible to understand why the young politicians in the LDP are so anxious to do America's bidding and send the Self-Defense Forces to Iraq.

There is, after all, no reason at all an island country such as Japan should go halfway around the world looking for opportunities to deploy the SDF abroad. The SDF are supposed to exist in order to defend Japan, aren't they? I was truly saddened and on the verge of tears when I saw the newscasts of SDF families looking on anxiously as their loved ones departed for Iraq.

Japan has gotten by so far without teaching its young people the horrors of war. The educational system has created a hear-no-war, see-no-war, and speak-no-war climate. This makes it all the more imperative that we preserve Article 9 with its pledge to the entire world that Japan will never again wage war.

(interview-based)

☐■☐ Reinterpretation Is Needed to Allow Female Emperors

Mori Youhei

Mori Youhei is a journalist.

Born in 1964. Graduated from Kyoto University Faculty of Letters. Went to work for the *Mainichi* newspaper. Assigned to the city desk, covering Imperial Household Agency and Metropolitan Police Department. Currently Washington correspondent for the *Ryuukyuu Shinpou* newspaper and reports on the U.S. and on the Imperial Family for a range of magazines. Researched with extensive use of Japan's freedom of information law, his *Tennou-ke no Saifu* (The Imperial Family's Finances) (Shinchousha) drew particular notice.

WITH THE CONSTITUTION stipulating that the Emperor is the symbol of the state, the issue of Imperial succession – and especially the idea of opening succession to women – is a matter of intense concern for all of the people.

A poll conducted by the Japan Opinion Research Association (a voluntary collaboration by Kyodo Tsuushin member companies) in June 2002 showed 76% of the people agreeing with the statement that a female Emperor would be acceptable. Yet the discussion still seems to be going nowhere because all kinds of problems arise in working out the actual details. The fiercest sticking point seems to be whether or not to actually allow female succession. Because this is somewhat difficult to understand in the abstract, let me go into some specifics.

The current Imperial House Law was passed by the Diet in late December 1946. At the time, the Emperor Showa's first-born, Princess Teru, had already married the eldest son of Prince Higashikuni Naruhiko and his wife Princess Toshiko. She and her husband, Prince Morihiro, had two children: a one-year-old boy, Nobuhiko, and an infant girl, Fumiko.

Had Article 14 of the Constitution and its principle that "there shall be no discrimination ... because of race, creed, sex, social station, or origin" been strictly applied, succession would have passed to the Emperor's first-born regardless of gender. In this case, the order of succession would have been (1) Princess Teru, (2) her son Prince Nobuhiko, (3) her daughter Princess Fumiko, (4) then back to the Emperor's other children with Princess Taka and (5) Princess Yori before getting to the current Emperor (6), Prince Akihito, who was then only 13 years old. In effect, the succession would have gone through Princess Teru to Prince Nobuhiko and the Imperial line would have seemed to sidetrack into the Higashikuni line.

This is why the conservatives with their emphasis on the weight of tradition were aghast at the idea of female succession. Because Princess Teru's father was the Emperor Showa, it could be argued that she was a girl of the male line, But Nobuhiko's father was Prince Higashikuni, meaning that he was only related to the Emperor Showa on his mother's side, thus making him a male of the female line. It was thus thought this succession would have entailed a change of dynasty.

Of course, it could also be argued that Princess Teru had already gotten married into another family – similar to being adopted – and had thereby forfeited her place in the line of succession. Similarly, it could be argued that when it comes time for Princess Aiko [daughter of the current Crown Prince] to marry, her husband could marry – be adopted – into the Imperial family such that their offspring would still continue the Imperial family line even though there might be a female Emperor for a while.

However, all eight of the female Emperors in Japanese history have been women of the male line. Except for Saimei and Genmei, both of whom had the distinction of being married to an Emperor or a Crown Prince, none of the children of these female Emperors succeeded to the throne. Thus there is no precedent for female succession. It has always, albeit at times with the help of adoption, been a male line "unbroken for ages eternal."

Appearing before the subcommittee meeting of the House of Representatives Constitution Study Committee on February 5, 2004, Constitutional scholar and Kyushu University Professor Emeritus Yokota Kouichi said that, while he is open to the idea of female succession, "I must point out the potential problem in that there is a strong possibility that having a female Emperor might end up weakening the ability of the throne to serve to unify the people. The basis of the throne's authority is that the throne has fundamentally been held by a male of the line for ages untold, and it is thus important we not allow female succession to contaminate this sacred bloodline and weaken this claim."

The old *ie* system, in which the family was a male-dominated institution and males carried on the family name, was abolished with the enactment of the postwar Civil Code. But there is still a strong strain within Japanese society that emphasizes the *ie*, and many of these people find their support and solace in the Imperial Household.

On the other side of the argument, there are also those who hope that legalizing female succession will undermine gender discrimination, change the *ie*-based consciousness, and hence lead to a society in which men and women participate as equals. This is evident in the question independent Diet member Takahashi Kiyoko posed at the February 1, 2001, meeting of the House of Councillors committee on ensuring equal rights for women. She asked: "Even as Article 14 of the Constitution clearly prohibits gender-based discrimination, the Imperial House Law clearly discriminates between men and women. It stipulates male-line succession, which is gender-based discrimination. In fact, the Imperial House Law says that only a male child of the male line may succeed to the throne. Is there any reasonable basis for this?"

The problem is that there are two very different groups voicing support for a female Emperor: the traditionalists who are willing to accept this as a last resort in order to maintain the continuity of the throne and the equal-rights advocates who take a feminist stance in calling the principle of male primacy into question.

The traditionalists thus want to consider reinstating the Imperial princes, abolished in the wake of defeat, to minimize the possibility of a female Emperor. Even though they are willing to put up with a female Emperor once in a while, they are looking for ways to make this as rare an occurrence as possible. They are, for example, looking at the possibility of changing the order of succession so that Prince Akishino and Prince Katsura (from a collateral branch) would be higher in the line of succession than Princess Aiko. Yet the equal-rights advocates will have none of this and insist that there should be absolute equality and gender-blindness in the succession.

Article 2 of the Constitution says simply, "The Imperial Throne shall be dynastic and succeeded to in accordance with the Imperial House Law passed by the Diet." The key concept here is "dynastic." In the past, the government has taken the position that this does not include the female line. So if Japan is to accept a female Emperor, the Constitution – or at least the government's interpretation of it – will have to be changed. This is expected to be another major issue of contention.

☐■☐ Article 9 Embodies an Essential, Universal Principle

Murayama Tomiichi

Murayama Tomiichi is a former Prime Minister.
Born in 1924 in Oita Prefecture. Served as Director on the House of Representatives Budget Committee, Japan Socialist Party Diet Affairs Chief, Member of the
JSP Central Executive Committee, and more. Selected as Prime Minister in June
1994, heading the coalition government formed by the Liberal Democratic Party,
Japan Socialist Party, and Sakigake party. Resigned in January 1996 and retired
from politics in 2000.

STUNG BY A vote of no-confidence, Prime Minister Miyazawa Kiichi dissolved the House of Representatives in the summer of 1993. Following the
election, a collection of minor parties joined together to form a government
with Hosokawa Morihiro at its head. When he resigned in April 1994, Hata
Tsutomu formed the successor government. This was a difficult time of great
flux, and in June 1994 I ended up designated as Prime Minister soon after the
Japan Socialist Party, which I headed, formed a coalition including the Liberal
Democratic Party and the Sakigake party.

I responded to questions in the House of Representatives the next month,
July 1994, by saying, "I believe the Constitution allows us the Self-Defense
Forces constituted as the minimum organization needed for our self-defense
and dedicated to an exclusively defensive role." This was not only my position as head of the JSP but was common ground shared by the three coalition
partners. As such, it articulated my answer to the difficult question of what
to do as Prime Minister and as the legal heir to the unwelcome political heritage bequeathed by previous administrations. It was a bitter compromise,
recognizing the impossibility of jettisoning prior policy and resolving this
issue at a single stroke.

Understandably, there was much acrimonious debate at the JSP's national congress that September. Yet in the end, we adopted the basic policy position that the SDF are permissible under the current Constitution and should be recognized as the minimum structure necessary for Japan's defense. From the end of the war until today, Japan has been able to continue as a nation of peace without going to war because of the many peace-loving people who used Article 9 as a bulwark against dangerous revisionist impulses, mounted widespread antiwar campaigns, and worked assiduously to nip conflict in the bud. Many people carried on the tradition of giving life to the Constitution's lofty ideals, and I like to think that I was also part of this movement after my postwar demobilization. Thus I can understand how my statement in the Diet was a grave disappointment to many JSP supporters and other activists and ordinary people who had fought to preserve the peace Constitution.

Looking back, the LDP politicians who ruled for so long after the war re-interpreted Article 9's renunciation of war for their own ends and worked assiduously to enlarge the SDF, to upgrade their capabilities, and to expand their mission. Indeed the LDP line has been that the Constitution does not re-nounce the right of self-defense, that the UN Charter explicitly recognizes the sovereign right of self-defense, that the Constitution simply prohibits waging war on another nation and possessing military force for the purpose of wag-ing such war, and that the Constitution thus allows a self-defense capability so long as it is intended solely for defense.

Upon reflection, it is clear that the confusion over the meaning of Article 9 has been engendered by those who would amend the Constitution to fa-cilitate remilitarization and that, even as they hid their ultimate intent, this confusion served as the logical battering ram for reinterpreting the Consti-tution to suit their convenience and put the Constitution's supporters on the defensive. And all the while the debate raged, the SDF grew bigger and bigger until those who would amend the Constitution could point to the SDF and argue, in an astonishing inversion of priorities, that the Constitution is out of touch with current realities. This was, it must be added, fueled by strong U.S. pressure as it sought to prevail in the Cold War.

When World War II ended, sincerely determined efforts were made to find some way to save the world from the scourge of repeated war. It was in this context that the Constitution was born, and it was in this context that the JSP made unarmed neutrality the bedrock of its security policy. Yet the objective conditions changed, and debate within the party came to focus on whether the SDF should be seen as constitutional or unconstitutional. Paralleling this, popular opinion regarding the SDF also underwent a gradual change, and recent polls show 70–80 percent approving the SDF's existence, including their use as needed for natural-disaster relief. Many proposals were put forth for restructuring, shrinking, and otherwise reforming the SDF, but it proved impossible to actually submit a bill calling for repeal of the SDF Law and excessive energy was spent arguing whether the SDF were Constitutional or not.

With the collapse of the Berlin Wall in 1989 and then of Cold War structures shortly thereafter, I felt it necessary to achieve closure on the assessment of the SDF's role and its compatibility with the Constitution. Ideology was on the decline, the historic three-party coalition government was formed, and I was designated Prime Minister. Even admitting the constraints imposed by the fact that I was a coalition Prime Minister, I wondered if there was not something I could do here. At the same time, the JSP, which should have provided the core bedrock for the coalition, was shaken by efforts to form a new party. Coincidentally, this was also the 50th anniversary of the war's end. Thus I released an official statement as Prime Minister expressing my remorse and apologies to all of the peoples of Asia for past Japanese aggression and colonialization. This statement was at one with my position on the peace Constitution, and I think it was consistent with my basic position on what Japan could and should do to build better international relations. Subsequent administrations have since reaffirmed this statement, and it was a clear statement of my creed having lived though the war and looking at the 50th anniversary of the war's end.

In the decade since I left the Prime Ministership, I have retired from electoral politics but remain deeply worried as a concerned citizen about how a way has been found to send the SDF overseas and about the frighteningly active campaign to amend the Constitution to recognize the right of collective self-defense and make Japan a "normal" country able to wage war unimpeded. Japan's peace Constitution is grounded in universal principles forged so that all humanity may live better in the 21st century. I am proud of the fact that Japan has been able to learn from its history, has vowed never to repeat the evil, and has lived in peace with all nations free of war for the 59 years since the war's end. And I believe that when amending the Constitution is put on the political calendar and the people come to actually cast their votes, the people will have the good sense to opt for peace for Japan and all the world, will make the right decision for posterity, and will not allow Article 9 to be amended.

□ ■ □ Guaranteeing the Victim's Right of Redress

Nakajima Hiroyuki

Nakajima Hiroyuki is an author and lawyer, and Executive Director of the Soft Air Gun Safety Council.

Born in 1955. Graduated from Waseda University Faculty of Law. Passed the bar exam in 1985. Well versed in criminology, victim studies, and U.S.-Japan comparative jurisprudence. While working as a lawyer, won the 1994 Edogawa Ranpo Prize with *Kensatu Sousa* (Prosecutor's Office Investigations). Among his other works are *Ihou Bengo* (Illegal Defense), *Shihou Sensoo* (Judicial Wars), and *Dai-ikkyuu Satsujin Bengo* (Defending Capital Cases) (all Kodansha). Originated the popular *Hokaben* cartoon series for Kodansha.

IN THINKING ABOUT the Constitution, I would like to look at what rights crime victims have under the Constitution, with special attention to their succor and the idea of the state's responsibility.

The current Constitution is criticized for being overly solicitous of the rights of the people committing the crime, be they suspects, defendants, or prisoners, but slighting the rights of victims. And it is true that the Constitution has a number of conspicuous provisions to guard the rights of people who may be on the wrong side of the law, from Article 31 on due process through Article 38's protection against self-incrimination. However, these protections for suspects and criminals are all restrictions on the state's power to punish wrongdoers, and none limits or even touches upon victim rights. This is a consequence of the importance the Constitution lays on human rights (including those for suspects and criminals), and it would be wrong to see this as slighting the rights of the victims. In fact, the Constitution is very much aware of victims' rights.

What, then, are the rights of crime victims? Very simply, they have the right of revenge. This right – to do unto others as they have done unto you or yours – is one of the oldest rights in history. The specific form has changed and evolved over the years, but the Code of Hammurabi, said to be the oldest known law, codified the ancient eye-for-an-eye idea of revenge, and this found reflection in Japan in the Edo-era codes recognizing the right of the victim's family to exact revenge in equivalent form. Indeed, this concept is still alive and well in today's laws.

Today, this right of revenge is couched in terms of seeking financial redress and reimbursement – it is a capitalistic revenge. Capitalist society is a utilitarian society in which all values are expressed in monetary terms, and the victim's right of revenge is no exception to this rule. Revenge is exacted by taking money from the perpetrator. While this is expressly covered in Article 709 of the Civil Code (the right to seek indemnification for illegal behavior), it is more basically covered by Article 13 of the Constitution on the right to the pursuit of happiness, because restoring the rights of the victim is a way of preserving the individual's rights. And because the victim's rights are embodied in the Constitutional right of revenge, the victim is able to sue for indemnification without regard to the rights of the wrongdoer.

Even so, many people who commit crimes do not actually have the means to indemnify the victims. The state seeks to punish the criminal in criminal court, but it claims that indemnification is a civil-court issue between the criminal and the victim and not something that involves the state. Yet this ignores the fact that the most basic duty of the state is that of protecting the lives of the people. Side by side with the state's obligation to ensure public safety, each individual also has the right of self-defense. In this age, when wrongdoers may well be armed with knives or guns, it would make sense from a self-defense perspective for people to be similarly armed to protect their families and themselves. A knife for a knife, a gun for a gun. It may even be you need a machine gun to hold off a gang of armed robbers. Yet that way lies America, with its 20 million guns in private hands and its danger-fraught society.

If Japan is to avoid turning into such a shoot-'em-up society, both sides have to honor the social contract under which the people agree to go unarmed and defenseless and the state agrees to provide them all necessary protection. The reason the people fall victim to criminal elements is that the state is not holding up its end of the contract. In legal terms, the state has been negligent in fulfilling its duty to protect them. Hence the state has an obligation and responsibility to assist in seeking redress (indemnification) for crime victims.

Given this, what is to be done? Counter-intuitively, I would suggest that the legal code turn the clock back a hundred years – to a time when the Criminal

Code and the Civil Code were not completely separate and when a criminal case could also include consideration of the civil case for indemnification (as an ancillary suit). With this system, the victim did not have to find and pay a lawyer and was able to have the evidence that was presented in the criminal court also considered in the civil suit. With the adoption of the modern concept of human rights after the war, the Criminal Code and the Civil Code were completely separated and the idea of ancillary suits, which had been so useful in winning redress for victims, was abolished as "a relic of the past." As a consequence, we had the mind-boggling situation of redress for victims being sacrificed in the name of modern human rights. We should take another look at the good relics from the past and reinstate the provisions for ancillary suits.

In the case of criminals without the wherewithal to pay indemnification, it might be useful to consider something along the lines of the debtors' gaol (a Civil Code prison) that existed in Victorian England to imprison people who could not pay indemnification as mandated by the civil courts. At the same time, we should fundamentally rethink the way our prisons work. The United States has a system of privately-operated prisons where factories within the prisons mass-produce goods for the commercial market – and this has evolved into a big business. Japanese prisons are all state-run, and the emphasis has traditionally been less on redress for the victims than on rehabilitation for the convicts. While there are woodworking and other craft shops as a form of therapy for prisoners, these are not very productive, are not engaged in mass production, and certainly do not make any money. But if the prisons were turned over to the private sector and turned to mass production for profit maximization, it would then be possible to use those profits (in addition to withholding from prisoner salaries) to indemnify victims. And criminals who do not pay indemnification even after they get out of prison could be thrown into debtors' prison and forced to pay. This would give new meaning to the phrase that flows so glibly from criminals' lips: I will pay for this for the rest of my life.

Crime is no respecter of person, and anyone can be a victim today. Thus the priority in criminal court cases should be not on rehabilitating the criminal but on finding redress for the victim. This is an important Constitutional issue.

(interview-based)

☐■☐ Protecting the Individual from the State

Nakajima Ramo

Born in 1952. Graduated from Osaka University of Arts Broadcast Department. Drew attention for his "Akarui Nayami Soudanshitsu" (Personal Consulting with a Smile) column, which ran in the *Asahi* newspaper for ten years. Won the 1992 Yoshikawa Eiji Prize for New Writers with his *Kon'ya, Subete no Baa de* (Tonight at Bars Everywhere) (Kodansha) and the 1994 Mystery Writers of Japan Award for Best Novel with *Gadara no Buta* (The Swine of Gadara) (Jitsugyou no Nihon-sha). Died in July 2004.

READING THE JAPANESE Constitution carefully and attentively, I find it to be a robust and reassuring document.

In fact, I am currently thinking of going to court based upon the provisions of this Constitution. And if I do, the defendant will be the Osaka Detention Center with its nearly sadistic, feudal system.

But let me start from the beginning. A little after noon on February 4, 2003, 11 narcotics agents from the Ministry of Health, Labour and Welfare burst into my home. They seized 6.9 grams of hashish and small amounts of mushroom that I had in my refrigerator. At 2:40 pm the same day, I was charged with violating the Cannabis Control Law and placed under arrest.

That is when the problems began. The Osaka Detention Center, where I was incarcerated, absolutely refused to allow me to have or take the regular medication that was keeping me alive. This was a major problem. I am subject to severe manic depression and insomnia. At times, the depression plunges me into very suicidal thinking. One time, for example, I was about to jump to my death and it was only sheer luck that my manager showed up and stopped me. So I was on medication – taking a major tranquilizer three times a day and three Rohypnols every night for my insomnia.

Yet the guards at the Osaka Detention Center told me they would not let me have any medications that had not been prescribed by the Center physician. Just for the record, it should be noted that this medication had been prescribed by a psychiatrist at Osaka City General Hospital. It was absurd that I would not be allowed to take medication that had been duly prescribed by a licensed physician. Yet I was not, and, as I feared, the stress of incarceration and questioning made me extremely anxious, gave me insomnia, and pushed my blood pressure into the stratosphere. Of course, I explained my situation to the people at the Osaka Detention Center and appealed every day for a medical appointment and a prescription. But they obviously had no intention of calling in a qualified psychiatrist. Every time I asked when I would be able to see a doctor, the answer was always "who knows?"

Early on my fifth morning of incarceration – February 9 – when I was huddled in my blanket trying to bear the 4° cold – things came to a head. Literally. I heard a loud "sheeeen" buzzing like a swarm of cicadas in the very center of my head. This was soon followed by excruciating pain radiating out from the center of my face as though a steel band about 4cm wide were being tightened around my head. This was clearly a precursor to a stroke. If left untreated, I could easily end up language-impaired or half-paralyzed – if I did not die first. But when I called for help, I was told there were no doctors or nurses on call because it was a weekend. So I told them, "In that case, handcuff me and take me to the emergency ward at the Osaka Police Hospital. There's no time to lose."

I was so insistent that even the guard started to worry, coming out and, by all appearances, going to ask for instructions from his superior. So I thought I would finally get to see a doctor. Yet my relief was short-lived. When he came back five minutes later, he dashed my hopes. "No way. Rules don't allow it."

About 1:00 the next afternoon, I finally got to see a doctor. When he took my blood pressure, the systolic (high) blood pressure was 230. The doctor blanched at this and quickly gave me a vasodilator to put under my tongue. Had my blood pressure gone over 250, I have no doubt I would have died. And I am sure it was very close to the 250 mark when I was railing at the guard the previous morning. I was on the brink – the cusp – between life and death. I am as certain of this as I have ever been of anything. It was the first time in my life that I had been exposed, a naked individual, to the full might and authority of the state. And it is not too much to say there was a very real risk the state would kill me.

This is why I, Nakajima Ramo, have made up my mind to file criminal proceedings against the Osaka Detention Center charging them with "attempted murder by gross negligence due to the inadequacy of their medical provisions." These (in)actions by the Osaka Detention Center are in violation of Article 25's right to life and Article 13's right to the pursuit of happiness.

I plan to seek four main things in court:

- Prompt improvement of the medical care (including 24-hour care with doctors and nurses available on three shifts),
- Legal discipline of the people responsible,
- Compensation in the amount of ¥300 million plus legal fees as indemnification for their having pushed the plaintiff (me) to the brink of death, and
- Inspections of and improvements to the operations of all holding facilities, detention centers, and prisons throughout Japan.

What a wonderful Constitution this is that it affords me grounds for boldly making such sweeping demands of the state. Having used up at least one of my nine lives there, I am now gearing up to strike back at the Osaka Detention Center. It is a good feeling.

(compiled from author materials)

☐■☐ A Greater Regard for Inventors' Rights

Nakamura Shuuji

Nakamura Shuuji is Professor at University of California at Santa Barbara.
Born in 1954. Following graduation from the University of Tokushima Graduate
School, went to work for Nichia Corporation in 1979. Was first in the world to produce commercial high-brightness blue LED. Retired from Nichia in 1999. Assumed
present position in 2000. Took Nichia to court over patent ownership and royalties;
the suit still pending in the Tokyo High Court. Among his works is *Ikari no Bureikusuruu*
(Breakthrough of Wrath) (Shuueisha).

THE CONSTITUTION HAS never meant that much to me, inventor that I am,
but since I am living in the United States now, I thought I would compare the
Japanese and U.S. Constitutions. And since I invented the technology that
made the blue LED possible, I wondered how the two countries would regard
that invention.

In fact, there are very considerable differences. To start with, the U.S.
Constitution – the basic law of the land – has a provision specifically on inventions. Clause 8 of Section 8 of Article 1 secures for inventors the exclusive
right to their discoveries. This statement of exclusive rights means that the
invention belongs to the person who invented it. Indeed, this is a universal
rule, and Japanese law says essentially the same thing. It just does not say it
anywhere in the Constitution. So the fact that the U.S. includes this in the
Constitution is a major difference from Japan. It means that the state's stance
toward inventors and inventions is different. The U.S. places more emphasis
on inventions and discoveries than Japan does. This is important for researchers and engineers.

Patent law is also very different in the two countries. U.S. patent law is famed
for being somewhat of an outlier in the international community – particularly in assigning priority to the first to invent. For example, if there are two

very similar inventions, Japan and Europe would recognize (grant the patent to) the first one to file a patent application. This is called first-to-file. By contrast, the U.S. contends that the date of filing is not that important and recognizes the first to invent.

In Japan, even if you are first to have a new idea, even if you are first to invent something, that is all for naught unless you are also first through the door with your patent application. But in the U.S., if you can demonstrate with your laboratory notes or otherwise that yours was the prior invention, you have priority even if you are not the first to file. Yet it must be admitted that there is considerable potential for problems in determining the order of events because the examiners and courts will give credence even to lab notes and napkin jottings.

I teach at a U.S. graduate school, and watching how students behave, I can see all kinds of advantages to the first-to-invent system. For example, say I have everyone do a certain experiment. They all do the experiment and note the results in their notebooks. So far, this is the same as what would happen at a Japanese university, but what happens after the lab session is different. In the U.S., they come and ask me to sign their notes. This they do because even the seemingly most trivial experimental results or discovery could conceivably lead to a major breakthrough invention. Having me sign their notes certifies what they did and when they did it, which may be something they would want to assert later. They understand this.

It is not only students. People also keep meticulous notes at corporate research laboratories, and Americans are very much aware of patents and other intellectual property rights. It is no accident that venture capital and venture business start-ups have boomed in the U.S., and this has had a major impact on the economic and technological potential. In this climate, both students and corporate researchers are eagerly looking forward to the day they can start their own companies. It is not at all uncommon for even a minor invention or discovery to spark a new start-up.

Knowing how rich you can get, everyone is sweating and scheming to launch a successful start-up so they can cash in on the initial public offering (IPO). The American Dream rules, and the U.S. first-to-invent system is thus a major force motivating researchers and engineers in their quest for new discoveries and inventions. I believe that this awareness has been a major factor in sustaining and enhancing America's inventiveness and technological prowess.

Japanese spending on research and development is among the highest in the world, Japan is technologically competitive, and Japanese patent applications easily lead the pack. Yet these advantages – money, technological prowess, intellectual property, and more – do not necessarily translate into actual business opportunities.

Almost without fail, Americans accept that the important thing is not when you filed the patent application but when you had the idea or made the discovery. By contrast, in Japan, not even many scientific researchers understand the basics of patent law and inventor rights. This difference probably arises from differences in the educational systems. In the U.S., junior high school and high school students learn about the patent system and inventing. In Japan, not even very many graduate-level classes touch upon the basic tenets of patent law and the filing procedures. When I was a student, for example, we were taught nothing on the patent system. Of course, now we have university spin-offs and industry tie-ups, but even so, I doubt many science students understand what is involved here.

Yet knowledge of the Constitution and the laws can be a major asset for researchers and engineers, and I hope they will understand this. I have taken my former employer to court, but I could not have done this if I had not known anything about patent law. Awareness of intellectual property rights is linked to international competitiveness. With so many corporate executives and educators hoping that researchers and engineers remain ignorant of these things, I fear for Japan's future.

☐■☐ The Constitution's Life-and-Death Significance

Nakamura Tetsu

Nakamura Tetsu is a physician, Peshawar-kai on-site representative, and PMS (Peshawar Medical Services) Director.

Born in 1946. Has treated Afghan and other refugees in Pakistan, Afghanistan, and elsewhere for Hansen's Disease (leprosy) since 1984. Also active in projects to revitalize arid regions by supporting irrigation and agricultural projects. Among his works are *Isha Ido wo Horu* (Doctors Digging Wells) and *Henkyou de Miru, Henkyou kara Miru* (Treating Patients in an Alien Land, the View from an Alien Land) (both Sekifusha).

AS A JAPANESE living abroad for the last 20 years, I have experienced firsthand the benefits of Article 9. The richer a nation becomes, the more likely it is to resort to force in pursuing its national interests. For 60 years, however, Japan has shunned this path. My patients at the Peshawar Medical Services Hospital near the Afghanistan-Pakistan border have long accorded Japan the same elevated status as Japanese have traditionally accorded Switzerland. To them, Japan represents peace and beauty.

These local sentiments about Japan are invaluable for my work in this difficult area and have often saved my life. I am grateful to the Constitution and can attest that I probably would have been killed if I weren't Japanese. Because of the Constitution, Japan cannot use force or the threat of force to settle disputes with other countries. People in Japan have no idea how very significant this ideal is internationally. So I want to use this opportunity to write about the practical consequences of the Constitution around the world.

The problem, however, is that the Afghan and Pakistani people are asking me if Japan has changed its mind now that it has sent the Self-Defense Forces to Iraq. All I can do is give them the convoluted reply, "Most Japanese are against the deployment, but the government went ahead with it anyway." I see their changing attitude toward Japan on a daily basis, and I am convinced that Japan will have ample reason to regret this action in 10 or 20 years.

In the course of my work, I have witnessed the deaths of many refugees and other people. In World War II, total Asian fatalities were over 10 million – including about 2 million Japanese combat personnel. How can Japan even think of sending the Self-Defense Forces into combat zones! Many say Japan's Constitution is out of touch with the new international order, but I say that it is the people intent on sending Japanese troops overseas who are out of touch with international reality. War is not some computer game. It is real people shedding real blood and dying real deaths.

Ever since the Self-Defense Forces' predecessor, the National Police Reserve, was established in the 1950s, there has been debate over its constitutionality. There have been arguments invoking realpolitik, arguments invoking idealism, and everything in between. But for the generation who actually experienced the war and its tragic aftermath, it is the Constitution that has to be credited for maintaining peace. Some people say that the Constitution was forced on Japan by the U.S. military, but I laud Article 9 as the distilled prayer of a generation that experienced war and wanted nothing more to do with it.

As the ranks of the war generation thin out and antiwar sentiment fades, I grow fearful about the unexpected resurgence of debate on Constitutional revision. Fewer and fewer people are acquainted with war's harsh reality. More and more people think of it as a game. To them, death is an abstract concept that applies to someone else.

To me, the arguments for revising the Constitution are arguments about realism by people who are divorced from reality and take peace for granted. "Defending the nation" and "protecting the people" sound like exemplary ideals, but deploying the Self-Defense Forces is a knee-jerk action.

Have Japan's politicians ever actually exerted themselves to preserve peace? Constitutional revision should be considered a last resort after all else fails. First and foremost, the effort must be made to work for peace. A state's primary responsibility is that of protecting the lives of its people. But Japanese leaders engage in diplomatic negotiations only halfheartedly; seizing upon "the war on terror" as their slogan, they are interested only in the national interest as manifested in the Japan-U.S. alliance. This approach only creates future problems. Peace is a fragile thing if we merely go through the motions of supporting it. More than anything else, it has been the experience of war that has kept Japan at peace.

The rest of the world sees Japan's renunciation of war as a means of settling international disputes (as symbolized by Article 9) as a measure grounded in reality, and this renunciation earns Japan much approbation and trust. Thus it is wrong to label the Constitution full of impractical and fanciful ideals, and it would be exceedingly dangerous if such thinking took hold and spread in Japan.

What is so important that the Self-Defense Forces must be dispatched to protect it? The answer lies in what we have been manipulated to believe: that Japan cannot survive without the United States. To be blunt, this is the idea that America's favor has to be curried whatever the cost, and a few lives lost in the process do not matter. I sense this terrifying ethos growing among the general public.

In brief, it is not possible to protect people by military power. This is my firm belief as someone who has worked unarmed in very dangerous places for 20 years. It takes courage to go unarmed. But in the end, this is the best protection.

(interview-based)

□ ■ □ A New Constitution for a New Era

Nakasone Yasuhiro

Nakasone Yasuhiro is a former Prime Minister.

Born in 1918 in Gunma Prefecture. Graduated from Tokyo Imperial University. Went to work for the Ministry of Home Affairs, where he served as Imperial Navy Paymaster Lieutenant-Commander and in other posts. Elected to the House of Representatives in 1947. Served as Minister of Transport, Director General of the Defense Agency, Director General of the Science and Technology Agency, and Minister of International Trade and Industry before becoming Japan's 82nd Prime Minister. Awarded the Grand Cordon of the Supreme Order of the Chrysanthemum in 1997.

THE CURRENT CONSTITUTION played a very important role in postwar Japan. It was, for example, under this Constitution that Japan achieved spectacular economic development. This was a major accomplishment. Yet, going on nearly 60 years since the Constitution was promulgated, a number of shortcomings have come to light. Many issues have arisen that cannot be adequately dealt with just by stretching and reinterpreting the Constitution. The time has come to create a new Constitution so as to create the Japan of tomorrow.

Particularly noteworthy is the fact that postwar Japan has fallen prey to a serious ailment that might be termed "the Japanese disease." When the war was lost and the Japanese spirit was devastated, Western thought poured in and distinctively Japanese norms and mores were lost. This affliction has become increasingly pronounced since the Soviet Union's collapse in 1991 marked the end of the Cold War.

With the end of the Cold War, nations and peoples that had huddled under the American or Soviet security blankets began to redefine and assert their own identities. Japan was no exception, yet Japan's response was belated

as system fatigue showed up on a number of fronts. This was, if you w.
epitomized by the implosion of the political, economic, and social bubbles.
Politics has been meandering for many years now, and the economy seems
impervious to recovery. Even society has been shaken by the sharp increase in
violent crime and the breakdown of the educational system. There is thus an
urgent need to overcome the Japanese disease so as to restructure and revive
politics, the economy, and society. And in so doing, there can be no ignoring
the present Constitution's failings.

A Constitution should be the very embodiment of and set the parameters
for everything – security, foreign policy, politics, the economy, social welfare,
education, tradition, culture, and more. Yet the Japanese Constitution as it
stands does not give adequate expression to these aspects – because it was
not written by the Japanese people themselves but was imposed on Japan by
the American Occupation forces.

That is why it is so important to have a sovereign Constitution created with
wide popular input and anchored in Japan's own identity. This will, I believe,
prove an important step on the path to curing the illness that has dogged
postwar Japan.

In seeking to repair the Constitution, Article 9 is bound to be one of the
main articles of contention. I would thus like to state my thoughts on it first.

I see no problems with leaving Paragraph 1 renouncing war as it is. Yet I have
my doubts about Paragraph 2's "land, sea, and air forces, as well as other war
potential, will never be maintained. The right of belligerency of the state will
not be recognized." Indeed, I believe there should be a clear assertion of the
state's right of self-defense, as well as a clear statement of the right of collective self-defense.

The right of collective self-defense is clearly recognized in the UN Charter
and the Japan-U.S. Mutual Security Treaty. There are thus major contradictions involved in the government's interpreting the Constitution as prohibiting the exercise of this right just because it is not explicitly mentioned.

Nations form alliances because they are not singly able to repel a potential
enemy attack. If Japan were unable to act in the event an alliance partner were
attacked, that would make any alliance involving Japan a lop-sided alliance
and would mean Japan would be the only party protected. No state can truly
be called sovereign that is under another's protection but has no obligation
to help its protector. Japan should obviously be able to exercise the right of
collective self-defense.

Of course, there are other places besides Article 9 that need to be amended and revised. There are new rights that need to be written into the Constitution – such as environmental rights and privacy rights – and the Preamble also needs to be rewritten to expunge the heavy influence of U.S. Occupation policy evident there. Even the procedures for amending the Constitution should be less rigid in order to make the Constitution easier to amend.

The Cabinet system also needs to be discussed and debated. I have, for example, long advocated direct popular election of the Prime Minister. The current Diet-based Cabinet system makes it very difficult for the electorate to tell who the Prime Minister will be and means that responsibility has no clear locus. Given the need for political leadership and clearly delineated responsibility, the system should be changed to provide direct popular election of the Prime Minister.

At the risk of repeating myself, I believe the current Constitution has played a major role in postwar Japan. Yet we cannot cling to the status quo forever. We need to re-ignite the Japanese spirit and create a new Japan. We need a new sovereign Constitution to lead Japan into the new age.

☐ ■ ☐ Getting Out of the Indifference Trap

Nemoto Ryouichi

Nemoto Ryouichi is Mayor of Yamatsuri, Fukushima Prefecture.

Born in 1937. Was elected mayor of Yamatsuri in April 1983 and is currently in his sixth term. Has drawn considerable attention for his refusal to connect Yama-tsuri with the National Resident Registry Network, his anti-merger declaration in response to the central government's efforts to encourage municipalities to merge and consolidate, and other efforts to assert local autonomy. Among his works is *Henkyou no Machi ga Nihon wo Ugokasita* (The Little Town That Transformed Japan) (Zaikai 21).

THE CONSTITUTION WAS not an issue in the mid-2004 House of Councillors election. Even though the government had just decided on the potentially unconstitutional course of sending the SDF to Iraq and joining the multinational coalition, the voters were not, on the whole, interested in discussing the Constitution.

Indeed, it seems the people are paying only half a mind to the Constitution. They seem to have no real awareness that their rights and even their daily lives are sustained by the Constitution. This was painfully evident in the national debate that took place over the Law Concerning the Protection of Personal Information. I made the decision as mayor not to link our town's data to the National Resident Registry Network (Juki Network) because I feared the Juki Network Law was but the first step on the slippery slope leading to a big-brother state. This law is a potential infringement of the right to privacy and other inherent rights, and suspicions are strong that it is unconstitutional. Given this, I could not see my way to blindly accepting it just because the Diet had passed it.

Yet these fears – this anxiety – failed to find an echo in public opinion, and most people seemed content to go along with whatever the government of the day said. This too is sadly indicative of the way the people are only half paying attention to the very Constitution that guarantees their rights.

Behind this indifference to the Constitution is a deep-rooted distrust of politicians and the bureaucracy. The people are disillusioned and believe that politics today is simply the politicians and bureaucrats jousting for personal gain. This is illustrated by the deep distrust in which the national pension system is held. While there is much talk of rewriting the Constitution, I do not believe there is any urgent need to amend the Constitution. Even Article 9, which is the focal point of the efforts by the proponents of amendment, seems fine to me the way it is, because all of the countries of the world are drawing closer together and the risk of an inter-state war now seems less than it has ever been.

I see no reason why either China or North Korea, two countries that are sometimes posited as potential adversaries, would go to war with Japan. China is busy working to become an economic great power, and there are forecasts that it will be the world's second most powerful economy, after only the U.S., by 2020. Why would China want to throw all of that away and go to war with Japan? And North Korea is just a small country in Northeast Asia in no position to wage war. These are both neighbors that Japan should be able to work with if it plays its foreign policy cards right. So why should Japan rewrite Article 9 and otherwise gird for war?

Another argument that the proponents of amendment make is to say that the current Constitution was forced upon Japan by the Americans and was not created in accordance with the popular will. I do not buy that. True, the Constitution was drafted by Kades and the other young people working for MacArthur and was heavily influenced by Allied, especially American, thinking. Yet reading the Preamble carefully turns up surprisingly little American ego. I do not think Kades and his cadre were so egotistical or ill-intentioned that they tried to have the Constitution reflect only American interests. Even today, Chapter III's statements about the rights and duties of the people are deeply moving and resonate profoundly.

Yet even so, as I said earlier, the people are only half paying attention to the Constitution and may well unthinkingly accept the idea of rewriting it. Calls for rewriting it are likely to grow stronger. If rewriting cannot be avoided, it should suffice to just rewrite the Preamble. Even then, it is essential that the people who want to rewrite the document explain clearly what kind of a Japan they propose and that there be full debate.

To suggest just a few points of discussion, if the Constitution *must* be amended, it would be well to include global environmental protection and the enhancement of local government. And greater flexibility might well be built into the provisions pertaining to the Emperor. For example, it might not be a bad idea to allow the Imperial Family a greater role in diplomacy and in representing Japan to the rest of the world. I have strong reservations about the current efforts to preserve the Imperial system if this means negating the individual personalities of the Imperial Family members and binding them hand and foot to a host of rigid rules and ritualistic roles.

It should also be possible to incorporate policies for dealing with the population bust – inevitably a key issue for Japan in the years ahead – in the Preamble. The fertility rate in Tokyo is now less than 1.0. What should Japan do given the prospect of too few children to reproduce the population? Solutions need to be found and found quickly. There are also predictions that the national debt will top ¥1,000 trillion by 2010. With this deterioration in Japan's fiscal balance, it will be impossible to preserve and enhance education, pensions, nursing care, and other basic government services unless these population trends are addressed and reversed. Rather than rewriting the Constitution to revise Article 9, it would be far better to take another look at the Constitution in terms of dealing with the population bust.

Yet overall, I do not think there are any major problems with the Constitution the way it is. The Constitution is not something to be rewritten lightly. Rather, we should be more worried about the fact that the people are generally uninterested in the Constitution and pay it only half a mind.

(interview-based)

□■□ Examining Past, Present, and Future

Nishi Osamu

Nishi Osamu is Professor, Komazawa University Faculty of Law.

Born in 1940. Completed the doctoral course in political science at Waseda University Graduate School. Specializes in comparative Constitutional studies. Among his works are *Kenpou Taikei no Ruikei Kenkyuu* (Pattern Analysis of Constitutional Forms) (Seibundou), *Nihonkoku Kenpou wo Kangaeru* (Thinking about the Japanese Constitution) (Bunshun Shinsho), *Nihonkoku Kenpou wa Koushite Umareta* (Birth of the Japanese Constitution) (Chuukou Bunko), and *Koko ga Hen da yo! Nihonkoku Kenpou* (Here's What's Wrong with the Japanese Constitution) (Ascii).

START WITH THE historical fact that the Constitution was created under pressure and with very heavy input from SCAP headquarters and the Far Eastern Commission. Writing at the time, University of Tokyo professor, member of the House of Peers, and Constitutional scholar extraordinaire Miyazawa Toshiyoshi had this to say: "Overall, the Constitution was not created at Japanese initiative, and those who assert that a modicum of autonomy was exercised are only deluding themselves."

It is worth citing one typical incident by way of illustration. Article 66 Paragraph 2's "The Prime Minister and other Ministers of State must be civilians" was inserted by SCAP at the insistence of the Far Eastern Commission after the Commission concluded that then-Prime Minister Ashida's insertion of "In order to accomplish the aims of the preceding paragraph" in Article 9 Paragraph 2 altered the Constitution to allow Japan to maintain military forces for its own self-defense. And then this had to be accepted even though there was no way of knowing what actual discussions had transpired within the Commission. Thus the debate in the 90th Session of the Imperial Diet was replete with non sequiturs and responses that indicated total disconnect. It is deplorable that the government – which bears ultimate responsibility for the Constitution – was not even privy to the thinking behind the document it adopted.

It is imperative that we relegate this drafting and adoption process to the dustbin of history and put things right by writing a new page in history in which we can take pride in having drafted and enacted the Constitution of our own free will and initiative.

The Constitution itself

I think it was very significant that we were given this Constitution with its espousal of the Emperor as symbol, its populism, pacifism, respect for fundamental human rights, and other ideals as a basic document to guide us as we toiled to rebuild from the postwar devastation. Yet even the Constitution – the supreme law of the nation – is still just a law, and it is essential that we constantly be questioning and verifying what it says. Ideally, we should be reviewing this every ten years after the first two decades. Such reviews would bring the Constitution closer to the people and would bridge the gap between the model and the actual.

In just another two years, it will be 60 years since the Constitution was promulgated. Japan is now a totally different country from what it was then. Environmental degradation rages unabated, the new information technology has given rise to an increasing need to protect the privacy of personal information, and startling advances in the life sciences have spawned new ethical quandaries. Such things were unimaginable when the Constitution was written.

Likewise, Japan is now one of the leading nations of the world, and it is unforgivable that it should think it can enjoy the benefits of peace and prosperity in splendid isolation. How can Japan take part in establishing and sustaining world peace while still sustaining its own peace? How can we create and share prosperity for the whole of the international community? These are all questions we should be asking and discussing seriously at the Constitutional level.

The current Constitution has served its purpose, and I believe we have entered a new phase preparatory to a new leap forward.

What should be done

There are two important considerations here. One is the need to establish a clear identity for Japan and the Japanese people. Japanese history, Japanese traditions, and Japanese culture all need to be explicitly included to affirm "the shape of the nation." The other is to look overseas at Constitutions elsewhere and then to bring that perspective to bear on our consideration of the Japanese Constitution. For example, what fundamental human rights do other Constitutions guarantee?

The Constitution should not be overly nationalistic, but neither should it be flavorless like distilled water. It is important that insightful thinking be brought to bear on this process. With the Constitution's limitations clearly evident, we need to discard the backward-looking thinking that clings stubbornly to this outmoded text and to bring the popular wisdom to bear in developing an even better Constitution for today.

Looking at the much-discussed Article 9, it is untenable that there should exist diametrically opposed interpretations on such issues as whether or not Japan may possess war potential for its self-defense and whether or not the SDF may be sent overseas on humanitarian relief missions. More than an abnormality, it is a national tragedy. I believe Japan should loudly and clearly proclaim to all the world that it is a country founded in and devoted to peace, that it possesses military forces to preserve the integrity of peace and stability, that these forces are firm adherents of the principle of civilian control, and that these forces may be deployed to establish and maintain international peace. This should all be explicit in the Constitution.

☐■☐ Getting Real about Gender Inequality

Okifuji Noriko

Okifuji Noriko is a nonfiction author.

Born in 1938. Graduated from Hokkaido University Faculty of Letters. Drew major attention with *Josei ga Shokuba wo Saru Hi* (When Women Leave the Workplace) (Shinchousha) on women in the workforce. Has been outspoken on women's issues, problems of the elderly, and other areas. Is Vice Chairperson of the Japanese Society for Caregiving for the Elderly and Director of the Women's Association for Better Aging Society, among other posts. Her most recent work is *Fuufu to iu Koufuku – Fuufu to iu Fukou* (Happily Married, Unhappily Married) (Shuueisha).

ONE OF MY friends lost her father to the war when she was only three. This was in 1943. As a result, her mother had to be both parents and the sole support for the whole family. When my friend graduated from junior high school and was thinking about continuing her education, her mother told her, "I will have to send your brother to high school, and we cannot afford to send you both. So I hope you'll give up the idea of going to high school." Not to be put off that easily, she took the high school entrance exam in secret. And when she saw her name on the list of people who had passed it, she thought, "There. That is enough."

Satisfied that she qualified, she was able to set the dream aside and go to work as a live-in seamstress at a clothing store. "I used to cry every time I saw former friends walk by the shop in their school uniforms."

Later she went to work as an aide at a home for old people unable to live independent lives, and she has now become the head of the team there. When her mother grew old and infirm, she – not her brother – was the one who took her mother in and took care of her. And her mother told her, "The one thing I regret is not sending you to high school. You wanted so to go."

Having lost her father to the war, she then found her educational opportunities limited just because she was a girl. Even after the new Constitution was promulgated, a lot of people still thought that women did not need any more than a basic education, and families who were poor decided who to educate in large part depending upon whether they were boys or girls.

Can we really say things have changed even today? According to a 2001 OECD report, Japan has the lowest percentage of female college graduates of any of the 24 countries surveyed. Indeed, it is no exaggeration to say that Article 26's "right to receive an equal education" remains a lofty-but-empty promise for many women.

Even when they receive higher educations, many of Japan's women are still full-time housewives. Both men and women seem unable to break out of the mental parameters that have bound Japan for over a century. A 2002 survey found 68% of women believing that men were favored in the workplace, and 37% of women and 47% of men adhering to a rigid stereotype of gender-based role differentiation in which the man is the breadwinner and the woman the homemaker. Whatever happened to the Constitutional ideal of being "equal under the law"?

Personally, I suspect the only reason I was able to go to a four-year university is that I did not have any brothers. And even then, my father did not want me to go to college. No matter how hard I worked, he said, "She's just some girl. She'll never amount to anything even with an education."

Even after I graduated, I kept being treated like "just some girl." Sexual harassment at work, perverts groping me on the train, men saying and doing the cruelest things without a second thought ... the indignities were boundless. Even my husband told me my going to work was an insult to his pride – he made me feel I was being wantonly neglectful toward my family and willfully indulgent toward myself. My very reason for wanting to work – to live my life to its fullest – was taken as a display of selfishness, and my husband did not help with the housework or the children. "Why should I?" he thought. "She's the one who wants to hold down a job." As a result, I was forced to perform multiple roles and even to sometimes endure violence at his hands.

Article 24 says that marriage shall be "maintained through mutual cooperation with the equal rights of husband and wife." These were just empty words in my case. When we got married, my husband was promoted to head of the household and I was relegated to domestic laborer.

The importance of family

Such attitudes account in part for the fact that so many women are marrying so late, and no doubt for the fact that the birth rate has been in unbroken decline for the past 30 years. Even today's shockingly low 1.29 fertility rate is striking testimony to the fact that there is only woefully inadequate support for women's concerns, that women are expected to play predetermined traditional roles, and that they cannot endure the excessive burden placed on them. On international comparisons, Japanese men stand out for how little time they spend on household chores. In the Scandinavian countries, where a concerted effort has been made to promote gender equality, men spend more time on household chores, the fertility rates are higher, and there are higher percentages of women working outside the home. Now more than ever, Japan needs to revise its thinking on gender relations and the home and needs to reaffirm and promote the idea of equality under the law. The Japanese government submitted its latest report to the United Nations Committee on the Elimination of Discrimination Against Women in July 2003. But if Japan is truly interested in being part of and contributing to the international community, it needs to go beyond filing reports and needs to transform itself into a more woman-friendly society by eliminating the increasingly serious forms of indirect discrimination.

Article 9 is obviously important, but even more important is for all of the people to make a determined effort to ensure that the "equality under the law" provisions apply to all of daily life. This is an essential part of creating a better future for Japan.

☐ ■ ☐ Do Rights Need to Be Added to Exist?

Okudaira Yasuhiro

Okudaira Yasuhiro is a University of Tokyo professor emeritus.

Born in 1929. Graduated from University of Tokyo Faculty of Law. Assumed present position after stints as professor at University of Tokyo Institute of Social Science and International Christian University, among others. Among his works are *Shiru Kenri* (The Right to Know) (Iwanami Shoten), *Doujidai e no Hatsugen* (To My Contemporaries) and *Naze Hyougen no Jiyuuka* (Why Freedom of Expression) (both University of Tokyo Press), *Kenpou Saiban no Kanousei* (The Potential for Constitutional Court Cases) (Iwanami Shoten), and *Kenpou ni Kodawaru, Kenpou no Souzouryoku* (Insisting on the Constitution: The Constitution's Imaginative Powers) (both Nihon Hyouronsha).

BACK IN THE late 1970s, I co-authored a high-school civics textbook and was assigned to write the "new rights" section. I remember writing something to the effect that a number of new rights have recently been asserted, including environmental rights, the right to personal privacy, and the right to know, even though they are not mentioned in the Constitution. This turned out to be a very timely passage, and other textbooks soon included similar sections. Yet I do not claim any special prescience. Legal scholars had already begun talking about these new rights, and I had simply reflected that discussion in the textbook I wrote.

Even so, there was a lot of grumbling from the education-caucus politicians and the Education Ministry bureaucrats about discussing these new rights in an official textbook. And when the texts came up for government appraisal and approval, the appraisal board took its cue from the higher-ups and came back to me with comments that can be summarized as: "There is a lot of talk about new rights, and some people are constantly claiming they have a right to this and a right to that. But there are no rights unless they are explicitly mentioned in the Constitution. So this whole rights debate is bunk." The powers that be are generally very hostile to the emergence of new rights and wary of the rights' assertion. My bout with the textbook appraisers was just one example of this.

Even the ordinary man on the street, not understanding the benefit to be gained from anything new, tends to react negatively to the emergence of new rights. I remember back in the early 1970s when "privacy" was a generally unfamiliar term not yet in the dictionaries or in people's working vocabularies. Even after the term started showing up in ordinary writing, one organization ran a survey on privacy that found a surprising number of people saying they still did not understand the word. And even among those who said they knew the term there were comments such as, "I know there are a lot of people making a lot of noise about privacy protection, but I suspect these are people who have something to hide and are not really on the up and up. Myself, I'm an upright citizen with nothing to hide, so I don't see any need to worry about guarding my privacy."

Today, with people collecting all manner of personal data and processing it this way and that, who – aside from exhibitionists and people who have no sense of any distinction between their private and public selves – can possibly think there is no need to worry about privacy protection? That said, the issue is further complicated by the wide range of meanings attributed to "privacy." In many cases, whether something is a privacy issue or not depends upon who is asking to see the information. For example, someone might be willing to disclose his personal information to one person but not another. And we might agree, albeit begrudgingly, to disclose some financial information to the tax office but not to the police or the judiciary. There are many different definitions, but the concept of privacy is generally thought to cover the essential factors that we share as human beings. This is the sense in which the term is used and the sense in which legal scholars interpret it.

Still this is all very complicated, and I apologize for getting off on what may look like a tangent. Yet the reason I have gone on at such length about this is that it impinges directly upon the rising chorus of calls for amending the Japanese Constitution. As everyone knows, the people who are calling the loudest for amending the Constitution have their sights set on Article 9. But the question is whether they will only propose amending Article 9 or whether they will propose other changes as well in an effort to win broader approval for the amendment process. (In fact, I suspect the discussion of adding new items to the Constitution has already contributed to winning greater support for amendment.) And, as already explained, the right of privacy is a prime candidate for addition to the Constitution. Not only is it a good idea (and I am all in favor of good additions to the Constitution), it is very well received by the general public.

Ever astute, the *Yomiuri* newspaper also included this in its proposed replacement Constitution of 1994. There the relevant passage (Article 19, Paragraph 2) on privacy reads, "All people have the right to be free of unwarranted interference with their private lives, their families, and their homes." Yet do we not have this right unless such a provision is added to the Constitution? And if so, what was the point of the arduous struggle since the Constitution's promulgation to secure such rights? What, in fact, do the people who want to add new provisions to the Constitution actually want to add? And what implications would the addition have on a difficult real-life legal case such as, for example, the suit to keep *Shuukan Bunshun* from publishing excerpts from Yu Miri's novel *Ishi ni Oyogu Sakana* (A Fish Swimming in Stones)? Those who argue that these new rights will not exist unless they are added to the Constitution are taking a very narrow view of the Constitution. And I fear they may be cutting their own throats in the process.

Personally, I am against amending Article 9, which is the real aim of those advocating amendment. Yet I have not gone into that issue here because, very simply, I feel it is more important to refute the idea that additions are needed – an idea that negates the possibilities for creative interpretation and that seeks to hide the real purpose (amending Article 9) in a cloud of obfuscation. I want to clear away the distractions so that we can focus on the real issues and our real enemies.

□■□ A Special Country Dedicated to Peace

Osanai Mieko

Osanai Mieko is a screenwriter and Director of the Japan Writers Guild.
Born in 1930. Graduated from Tsurumi Girls' Senior High School. Has worked on
many popular television programs, including NHK's Sunday evening prime-time
drama *Tobu ga Gotoku* (Like Flying) and TBS's *San-nen B-gumi Kinpachi Sensei*
(Kinpachi and His Ninth-grade Students). Has spent much of her time recently on
volunteer activities. The Japan Team of Young Human Power, of which she is Prin-
cipal, is actively building schools in Cambodia.

WHENEVER TALK TURNS to the Constitution, people on both extremes furl
their brows and take on a forbidding look. Why? Because the first thing they
think of is Article 9.

While there are still some dinosaurs in the Diet who would disagree, I think
it is safe to say that the Constitution is a contract between the people and the
state – a document setting forth the rights guaranteed us and the duties we
are expected to fulfill as citizens in a state in which the citizenry is sovereign.
Thus amending the Constitution is akin to tearing up a contract and rewriting it, but this is a contract that would not have been viable were it not for
Article 9.

Even if you subtract children from the total population of 130 million, I
wonder how many Japanese have given serious thought and study to the Constitution. Abysmally few, I fear. Before rushing to compel children to sing the
national anthem, educators should include the Constitution of Japan in the
elementary, junior-high, and high-school curricula.

The fact that people can live their lives without so much as a thought about
the structures by which their lives, freedoms, and property are protected is
indicative of how incredibly superficial their sense of happiness is. Yet why
do wrongful convictions and discrimination still exist in this rich country? I

wish everyone would study the Constitution and learn that the legal remedies lie therein. The beauty of the Preamble and the lofty ideals of the Constitution's spirit should guide all of the people in all we do.

"We recognize that all people of the world have the right to live in peace, free from fear and want." Realizing that I should not just be concerned with Japan's fate but should also be interested in other countries, and wanting to do something to earn an honored place in the international society, I went to the Middle East for the first time in 1990. This was just after Iraq had invaded Kuwait and triggered the Gulf crisis. It was also before the Peacekeeping Operations (PKO) Law was passed and before the Self-Defense Forces were sent overseas – a time when Japan was being bashed for its "checkbook diplomacy" even though it was making a considerable international contribution consistent with the Constitution. This bashing was the most blatant interference in Japan's internal politics – interference from countries that were only too happy to cash the checks Japan wrote. The recent rush to send troops to Iraq after Saddam Hussein was overthrown stemmed in large part from a desire to avoid a replay of this trauma. People complained that Japanese assistance was managed by faceless bureaucrats with no local presence. So I went to put a face on it – to personalize it. It was a very educational experience. I was 60 at the time.

There were large numbers of young people from all over the world working at the refugee camps set up for people fleeing Iraq. And many of them were very much in favor of the Japanese Constitution. "I like the Japanese system with its renunciation of war" and "You got rich because you were able to spend the money you didn't spend on the military on economic development" were just two of the comments I heard. It was the same in 1991 in refugee camps along the Iran-Iraq border. I had a very real feeling that the Japanese Constitution is known worldwide – and known as a far more wonderful Constitution than we give it credit for being.

Yet despite the Constitution's being held in such high esteem, there are some politicians who argue strenuously that Japan can never be fully accepted unless the SDF engage in combat as part of a multinational coalition. Does this mean that Switzerland, which is armed to the teeth but has adopted a porcupine strategy of avoiding war, is not accepted by the international community? Far from it. Instead, Switzerland is accepted by all the world as "a special country" and a special case. Japan should also be a special case by adhering rigorously to Article 9 – no matter how much this might offend the countries that export massive mountains of munitions and might displease the merchants of death.

Under the guise of humanitarian assistance, Japan has taken the initiative and sent the SDF to Iraq as part of the coalition of the willing. But if this is humanitarian assistance, there is no need for them to go in battle fatigues. Rather, given Japan's brink-of-bankruptcy situation and need to restructure almost everything, they should forgo spiffy new uniforms and go in ordinary work clothes.

In the refugee camps along the Iran-Iraq border and in the Somalian refugee camps in Djibouti, I met young German volunteers in good-looking work clothes. These were people putting in plumbing, doing wiring, and building facilities. They were professionals sent by their guilds. Wearing fatigues, the SDF in Iraq are inevitably seen as part of the occupation, which means that hostility to them increases daily. Indeed, veteran Japanese journalists have already been shot there.

Before he was killed, Hashida Shinsuke reported from Iraq on how the SDF were spending ¥100 million to provide water worth ¥2 million on the open market. I saw the same thing at the Takeo base in Cambodia in 1992. All of this was paid for by ordinary citizens fulfilling their contractual obligation to pay taxes, yet these are taxes paid in the expectation the money will be used wisely to banish "tyranny and slavery, oppression and intolerance for all time from the earth."

Thus I hope Japan can be a special country that, cherishing the Japan-U.S. alliance, will be able as a good and loyal friend to proffer honest advice to the United States, the world's only superpower, in the spirit of the Constitution to prevent global turmoil. There are some who claim my pacifism is unrealistic and ask what I would do were Japan attacked, but the adversary would not escape unscathed. Surely Japan has the necessary means to defend itself. Being of the generation that survived World War II, I feel it is all the more incumbent upon me to raise my voice today: Put an end to the killing and being killed. Why can't we live together in peace?

□■□ The Responsibilities of Democracy

Ryu

Ryu is a media personality.

Born in 1968. Graduated from Sophia University Faculty of Economics. Hired by Itochu in 1991. Quit Itochu in 1993 to be a rapper. Has also appeared on television as an interpreter. Did voice acting and was cultural director for Sony Playstation's *Pa Rappa the Rapper* in 1997. Has been on J-Wave's "Soul Train" since 1999 and is also a media producer working as "327."

I GREW UP in the United States. From age 4 to 18, I was just like any other American kid. In junior high, I had to memorize the Constitution like everyone else. This was a standard part of the eighth-grade curriculum. Amid much groaning, everyone learns the Constitution. But just like junior-high kids in Japan, I had no idea what it all meant. I just memorized it. That's the way things are in a classroom setting.

But that's not the way they should be. No way! Like I say on the radio, this is our country. It belongs to you out there reading this book just the same as it belongs to me. It's not just for the politicians. And because the Constitution is a codification of the rules intended to enhance and protect each and every person's happiness, it behooves us all to take another look at this Constitution and think about what it means.

In rereading the Japanese Constitution, I was struck anew with what a great country Japan is. The human rights that we take for granted, the Emperor, the basic approach to military conflict, the job of politicians – all of these things are spelled out in easy-to-understand language.

To be perfectly honest, I had never really sat down and read the Constitution seriously until the editors asked me to write a short essay on my thinking for this book. So my first reaction was an embarrassed, "What? The Constitution? Who? Me?" and I was very hesitant about agreeing to do this. But I suspect this would be the first reaction of any ordinary person asked to write something about the Constitution. The Constitution has a sort of forbidding air about it, and it's not something most people spend a lot of time reading and thinking about. But then I realized this is no attitude for me to take. It's nobody's Constitution but ours.

When I was in grade school in Los Angeles, we had very thoroughgoing practice in democracy. Even the elections for class president and the like were very realistic, with the candidates campaigning hard to win. Of course, this was grade school, and it was unlikely the class officers would have any real say in how the school was run, so the campaigns were largely symbolic, but the candidates did all kinds of things to get noticed and elected. One kid mooned his opponents during a campaign speech, another shaved her head, and another got a rock band together for the occasion. And of course we ordinary voters got all caught up in the excitement. The whole election process was there: running for office, campaigning, voting, and declaring winners and losers.

The same school had a Model United Nations program with students assigned to represent Japan, the United States, France, and other countries. Indeed, there were all kinds of programs encouraging people to speak out and engage in the clash of ideas all year long. And the result of this experience was that we kids were naturally interested in politics, the UN, and international affairs. We had a basic understanding of the issues, we had our own views, and we were interested in the news. I wonder if the same kind of practical training in democracy could not be done in Japan.

When I started going to high school, the school encouraged us to get part-time jobs. The student affairs office even helped arrange them because they saw it as practical experience and good training for real life.

Looking at this, I wonder if Japan really needs its elaborate system of entrance exams, or if something else would be better. And surely I am not the only one who suspects the Constitution provides hints on how to answer such fundamental questions.

One of the things I noticed after I moved back to Japan was that the flag had been in every American classroom but I seldom saw the flag in Japan. I would like to see more people flying the flag here. In fact, I suspect the Japanese flag is one of the easiest in the world to identify. It is very distinct. Everybody knows it is the Japanese flag. And I would like people to also know what Japan stands for and would like every one of us to have a distinctive identity informed by Japan's history and traditions.

I expect this is something everyone who has lived overseas understands, but people who have spent all their lives in Japan do not realize what strong recognition and what a good reputation Japan has overseas. We should never forget this, and when we go overseas we should be proud of being Japanese.

I know there is a rising clamor to amend the Constitution, and my own feeling is that it should be reviewed every so often and anything that needs changing should be changed. Of course, you want to think things through and not make any rash changes. And you don't want to change the things that should not be changed, such as the thinking on democracy and international peace, but anything that is irrelevant or dysfunctional should be axed. And of course the people have to be fully consulted and the results should reflect the popular mandate. After all, that's what the Constitution is all about, isn't it?

Underlying all of this is the realization that we can no longer sit back and wait for somebody else to do it. We have to make ourselves heard, have to discuss the issues, and have to make Japan the kind of country we want it to be. It is up to us.

□■□An Urgent Need for Reality-based Everyday Laws
Sakakibara Eisuke

Sakakibara Eisuke is Professor, Keio University Global Security Research Institute, and Former Vice Minister of Finance for International Affairs.

Born in 1941. Went to work for the Ministry of Finance in 1965 following completion of his graduate studies at the University of Tokyo. Received PhD in economics from the University of Michigan in 1969. Worked in International Finance Bureau and other bureaus and became known as "Mr. Yen." Retired from the Ministry in 1999. Among his works is *Bunken Kokka e no Ketsudan* (Decision for a Decentralized Government) (Mainichi Shinbunsha).

I DO NOT think there is any need for the Constitution to go into a lot of detail. It just needs to set out the basics. It should be kept as simple as possible. The 17-point charter written by Prince Shoutoku Taishi in 604 seems about right to me. Or follow the British example and leave it unwritten. So in that sense, I do not advocate amending the Constitution so much as I advocate doing away with it altogether.

I came to this conclusion as a result of my experience working as a Ministry of Finance bureaucrat. Even then, global structures were changing very quickly and there was a great diversification of people's thinking. But every time we tried to innovate and change the laws in response to these changes, we ran into all manner of Constitutional restrictions and found our hands tied. Changing the laws is an important part of structural reform, but it is very difficult to amend the laws in Japan. Not only is it massively difficult to ensure compatibility between the new law and all of the other interlocking laws, there is very little flexibility or leeway in the Constitution – the nation's fundamental law.

For example, one of the laws we wanted to revise when I was at the Ministry is the Coinage Law. This law was enacted back when Japan was on the gold standard and went into effect in the late 1890s. Stipulating that one yen shall be equal to 0.75 grams of gold, it is obviously a relic of an earlier era. We wanted to amend this law so that we would be able to issue commemorative coins, but when we actually sat down and tried to amend it, people who had been around the Ministry longer than we had told us this is a fundamental law linked directly to the Constitution. A number of them got very upset and told us in no uncertain terms not to fool around with it. Even though we eventually got it amended, the experience showed that it is very difficult to change even a moldy old law like this. Such is the reality of Japan's legal structure.

I believe the Constitution should be flexibly open to change in order to stay consistent with the times. Yet the procedure for amending the Constitution is exceptionally daunting. Jumping through all of the hoops would probably take about ten years. By the time the Constitution is brought up to date, it will already be out of date. The world is changing that rapidly. As a result, it seems impossible, for all practical purposes, to revise the Constitution and keep it compatible with global conditions.

My father had an inside look at the Constitution's creation. A reporter for Domei – Japan's international wire service until the end of the war – he was appointed secretary to the postwar Ashida Hitoshi Cabinet with responsibility for liaising with SCAP headquarters. Perhaps it was the fact that we lived in Kamakura, as did Ashida, that brought the two men together, but whatever the reason, Colonel Kades and the other young Occupation officers who drafted the Constitution were frequent visitors to our home in Kamakura. As everyone knows, Kades and the others drafted the Constitution in just nine days, without asking any Japanese what they thought. My father, who advocated remilitarization, frequently told us, "This Constitution is primarily a SCAP initiative. It should be amended quickly." He said this even though he was a personal friend of the drafters. Although I did not have any strong feelings on this issue then, my experiences in government convinced me he was right.

Because it is so very difficult to amend the Constitution, people have gotten around this by devising new interpretations rather than writing a new Constitution to meet the exigencies. Something like sending the SDF to Iraq, for example, should really require amending the Constitution. But given the impossibility of amending it, a re-interpretation work-around was devised to allow sending the SDF overseas. Yet it is the bureaucrats who have the power to interpret the laws, and I worry that this gives the executive inordinate power within the government.

What specific amendments would I like to see? To start with, I would leave the things that there is broad popular consensus on – e.g., popular sovereignty, respect for fundamental human rights, pacifism, and the Imperial institution – as they are. That said, Article 9 is a major focus of debate, and I think it should be rewritten while still preserving the spirit of the original – this because I think there is a de-facto consensus among the people in favor of possessing the military forces necessary for Japan's self-defense. In addition, I think we also need to revise, among other things, the provisions relating to the Cabinet, the Diet, and amending the Constitution. For example, I think a simple majority affirmative vote of the people should be sufficient for amending the Constitution, and there is no need to require two-thirds affirmative votes in both Houses of the Diet before an amendment can be put to referendum.

So my idea would be to build around these fundamental concepts and come up with a slim Constitution of 17 articles or so. Rather than go into any more detail than that, I would build in the democratic rule that other issues as necessary are to be debated by all of the people and decided by majority vote. The lesser laws can be written as needed.

Even so, even amending the Constitution would not mean things would change overnight. So personally, rather than spending a lot of energy trying to amend the Constitution, I would rather work to change the lower-level laws so as to respond better to the reality we face every day.

(interview-based)

☐■☐ The Significance and Limitations of "Normalcy"

Sakurada Jun

Sakurada Jun is Lecturer, Toyo Gakuen University School of Modern Management. Born in 1965. Graduated from Hokkaido University Faculty of Law. Completed the Master's course at University of Tokyo Graduate School of Law and Politics. Took current post following a career including a stint as policy advisor to a member of the House of Representatives. Winner of the first Yomiuri Rondan Shinjinshou (New Opinion Leader of the Year Award) and the First Seiron Fresh-breeze Award. Published works include *Kokka no Yakuwari to ha Nani ka* (What Is the Role of the State?) (Chikuma Shinsho) and *Kokka e no Ishi* (Determination Toward the State) (Chuukou Sousho).

"MY SWORD IS not for taking life. It is for giving life." So wrote Yagyuu Munenori, a martial arts teacher in the employee of the second Tokugawa shogun Iemitsu, in his *Heiho Kadensho* (Family Secrets of Swordsmanship). This is an eloquent statement of his approach to his art.

Discussion of revising the Constitution has traditionally focused on Article 9 – and hence on the military, the security treaty, and war in the broadest sense. Yet in considering the issue of war I am invariably reminded of this passage from *Heiho Kadensho*. The standard argument from those who oppose revising Article 9 has typically been that arms are intended to kill, that their possession leads to their use, and that it is therefore better not to possess arms at all so as to avoid their use. By contrast, those in favor of revising Article 9 have argued that arms are essential to Japan's defense and that going unarmed is an open invitation to subjugation. I would like to say a few words in favor of revision from this traditionalist standpoint.

That said, I feel it is imperative, now that it may actually be possible to revise the Constitution, to consider what kinds of arms Japan might bear and how they might be employed.

There has been increasing pressure on Japan over the past decade or so to shed its inhibitions and become a "normal" country – the thinking being that only by becoming a normal country will Japan be able to respond appropriately to the changes in the international situation following the end of the Cold War. The critical issues facing us since the end of the Cold War range from reducing the threat of terrorism to preventing the proliferation of weapons of mass destruction, reviving failed states, preserving the global environment, eradicating poverty, preventing the spread of contagious diseases, protecting human rights, and more. It is a very wide-ranging menu of problems. Among the most pressing transnational issues are those of reducing the threat of terrorism, preventing the proliferation of weapons of mass destruction, and reviving failed states, none of which can be effectively addressed unless Japan has the full accoutrement of capabilities accruing to a normal country. Still, there are others such as preserving the global environment and eradicating poverty for which military might, one of the characteristics typically defining the normal state, is essentially irrelevant.

At the same time, the very concept of "power" as it is used to back up initiatives the state may wish to mount in the international realm means more than simply the "hard power" typified by military and economic might; it also includes such "soft-power" aspects as information, public relations, culture, and other things that resonate with citizens of other countries and cause them to be favorably inclined to the country. Indeed, soft power is increasingly important. Even if Japan is able to revise its Constitution and achieve normal-country status, that step will only put the necessary conditions in place and will not in itself enable Japan to deal effectively with trans-border issues.

Thus it is important in promoting Constitutional revision that Japan be fully aware of the significance and limitations of normal-country status. And in this, I suspect it will also be essential for Japan to hark back to Yagyuu Munenori's dictum and declare that "this sword is for giving life." In fact, the most important thing, once Japan becomes a normal state with its own military force and the legal trappings necessary for the force's deployment, will be to ensure that Japan has a robust political culture that makes every possible effort to avoid deploying its military force. Even in sending the Self-Defense Forces to Iraq, there was great debate about whether or not to send them but too little discussion of what they could actually do there and how their efforts would be coordinated with those of the Foreign Ministry, NGOs, and other organizations so as to ensure that all of these efforts actually contribute to rebuilding Iraqi society. Lacking such substantive issues, the question of sending the SDF to Iraq became an all-or-nothing, yes-or-no question, which was a most unfortunate outcome. Such simplistic discussion is a far cry from the kind of political sophistication and deliberation needed if Japan is to work to ensure that it need never unsheathe its sword.

Even without referring back to *Heiho Kadensho*, Japan has a long martial-arts tradition, and it is understood as a matter of common sense that there are certain rituals, a certain decorum, and certain rules of engagement that should accompany any use of force. It would be a shame if this common-sense civility were lost in the rush to be a "normal" country.

☐■☐ No Substitute for Social Reform

Satou Kouji

Satou Kouji is Professor and Dean, Kinki University School of Law.
Born in 1937. Graduated from Kyoto University. Among his many positions are Director, Japan Public Law Association; Chair, Osaka Prefectural Privacy Protection Council; Member, Ministry of Justice Legislative Council; Chair, Law School Committee, Central Council for Education; and Chair, Advisors Council, Justice System Reform Promotion Headquarters. Among his works are *Kenpou to sono Monogatari-sei* (The Story of the Constitution) and *Nihonkoku Kenpou to Hou no Shihai* (The Constitution and the Rule of Law) (both Yuuhikaku).

1. THE DAY THE House of Representatives passed the draft of the Constitution of Japan in 1946, Ozaki Yukio, known as "the father of constitutional government," took the podium and gave a speech in which, according to page 505 of volume 35 of the minutes of the 90th Session of the Imperial House of Representatives, he said: "It would be a major mistake to favor this draft thinking that a good Constitution will make a good society. If a good Constitution were sufficient to save the state, there would be no failed states. A good Constitution can be created easily, but its implementation is difficult. Just as I remind you of this, so am I concerned about it myself." But belying his words, it is not that easy even to create a good Constitution. The current Constitution, which differs radically from the Meiji Constitution, was possible only because conditions were abnormal during the occupation. But as he said, even with a good Constitution, good implementation is another question.

2. Created against the backdrop of the tragic events that took place under the Meiji Constitution, the postwar Constitution had four major objectives: (a) to establish respect for the individual and protection for fundamental human rights, (b) to restore political authority, (c) to spread the rule of law, and (d)

to further policies of international harmony. All marked complete turnabouts from the principles underlying the Meiji Constitution, and this realization drove the work that was done at the same time to bring the laws and regulations into line with the new Constitution.

The question was one of implementation. To what extent would the new state seek to identify the causes of those tragic events and work faithfully and unfailingly to achieve the new Constitution's aims as part of "the age-old struggle to be free"?

Not only was it not easy to change people's thinking and behavior overnight; the central bureaucracy was left in place basically unchanged. True, postwar Japan seems to have undergone a major transformation with its new Constitution, and postwar history has been characterized by a relentless pursuit of prosperity and Japan's emergence as an economic power. Yet starting around 1990, with the end of the Cold War, the relentless tide of globalization, and the collapse of the economic bubble in Japan, it has become starkly obvious how very far removed Japanese politics is from the ideals envisioned in the Constitution, and there have been a surprising number of facets showing how much the situation resembles that under the old Meiji Constitution. To cite just a few examples, there is the government led by the executive (the bureaucracy) with all of the ministries and agencies having silo vision, a political system that depends on the bureaucracy and is noticeably bereft of leadership, the embattled and weakened role of law as epitomized by the phrase "20% justice" (meaning that the judiciary does only 20% of what it should do), the increasingly irrelevant trappings of local self-government, and a popular consciousness that might be summed up as a "flight from freedom" (as evidenced in the results of NHK public opinion polls conducted every five years showing that most of the people think the "right to life" is guaranteed under the Constitution while smaller and smaller percentages cite freedom of speech, freedom of assembly, and other fundamental rights). And then there is the postal savings system – so big it dwarfs any number of megabanks combined – that funnels massive amounts of money to special government corporations and other bodies while nobody notices that anything is wrong with this picture. And the fiscal deficit that grows and grows to mind-boggling levels, with billions of yen worth of new debt being issued every year.

3. Beginning about 1990 or so, "this decade" became "this lost decade," but it was also the decade in which efforts were made to advance political reform, administrative reform, devolution of authority to local governments, eco-

nomic structural reform, and other reforms. In June 2001 the government's Judicial Reform Council submitted a set of recommendations to the Cabinet. As noted by the Council, "What commonly underlies these reforms is the will that each and every person will break out of the consciousness of being a governed object and will become a governing subject, with autonomy and bearing social responsibility, and that the people will participate in building a free and fair society in mutual cooperation and will work to restore rich creativity and vitality to this country. This reform of the justice system aims to tie these various reforms together organically under 'the rule of law' that is one of the fundamental concepts on which the Constitution is based. Justice system reform should be positioned as the 'final linchpin' of a series of various reforms concerning restructuring of 'the shape of our country.'" That said, the Council put these judicial reforms forth as a single package under the rule-of-law ideal – a basic principle embodied in the Constitution – and argued that the reform package was the final link in the long series of reforms intended to reshape the Japanese state.

Because postwar Japanese Constitutional scholars devoted most of their attention to explicating the Constitution's fundamental ideals and were not as vigorous as they might have been in examining how these ideals could be actualized in society, they have not taken a clear stand on the plethora of reforms offered up over the last decade. Nishio Masaru has noted: "In Constitutional studies terms … it is most regrettable that interest has centered almost entirely upon the relationship between the Diet and the Cabinet and virtually no attention has been paid to the issue of government by a bureaucracy of appointed officials."

There are parts of the Constitution we should consider amending, but when the talk turns to wholesale rewriting, I am reminded of Ozaki's observation that it is easy to write a good Constitution but difficult to put it into practice. Have not all of our efforts over the last decade – including the political reforms, administrative reforms, judicial reforms, and many other reforms including the effort to shrink the bloated fiscal deficit – been directed, albeit belatedly, to laying the foundations for solving the many issues that confront us in the 21st century? The true worth of the Constitution has been very much in evidence in this decade of toil and torment.

□■□ Why Should We Trust Them This Time Around?

Satou Toshiki

Satou Toshiki is Professor, University of Tokyo Graduate School of Arts and Sciences. Born in 1963. Specialist in international sociology. Among his works are *Kindai- , Soshiki- , Shihon-shugi Nihon to Seiou ni okeru Kindai no Chihei* (Modern Horizons in Modernist, Structuralist, and Capitalist Japan and Western Europe) (Mineruva Shobo), *Noiman no Yume, Kindai no Yokubou: Jouhouka Shakai wo Kaitai Suru* (Neumann's Dream, Modern Desires: Deconstructing the Information Society) (Kodansha), *Fubyoudo Shakai Nihon Sayonara Souchuuryuu* (Japan's Society of Inequality: Good-bye to a Middle-class Nation), and *'00 Nendai no Kakusa Geemu* (One-upsmanship in the First Decade of the New Century) (last two both Chuuou Kouron Shinsha).

THERE IS ONE thing that always bothers me about the way people discuss Article 9. And no, it is not so much their political agendas. It is more that they do not discuss the real issues and that the discussion is always off on a tangent. The discussion always gets hijacked.

Rereading Article 9, I am reminded of the scene in Ootomo Katsuhiro's *Akira* in which Akira, a child who has nuclear-force powers, is kept in a hibernation device that takes its occupants down to near absolute zero and the Colonel says, "He is frightening – so terribly frightening that we keep him locked away."

Article 9 is often portrayed as a declaration of absolute pacifism, but that is a vast misreading. The Constitution exists paired as if at birth with the U.S.–Japan Security Treaty. Article 9 lives not because postwar Japan has not relied upon military force but because the military force it relied upon was American.

Article 9 does not renounce military force *per se*. It renounces Japanese military force. This has two faces – one looking outward and the other looking inward, and the philosophical basis for the inward-looking one is that the military always runs amok and takes over the state (i.e., becomes an enemy of the people). In effect, this argues that the military is akin to scirrhous cancer or the HIV virus. Even a small infection quickly spreads and ends up killing the host. So it is essential not to be infected. This is the absolute in Article 9's absolute pacifism. More than renouncing military force, Japan washed its hands of its military. In effect, Japan gave up on the idea of civilian control.

Given this, it then becomes obvious what fundamental issue the debate over Article 9 is skirting and hiding: Japan's disastrous history with civilian control. Or, more precisely, the possibility of repeating that history. The military always and inevitably runs amok. So it is not the people's fault that the Japanese military ran amok. That's what militaries do. It is the military's fault – military force's fault. If it is anyone's fault, it is the military professionals' fault. So no blame attaches to the ordinary Japanese, most of whom were civilians. This is a very comforting logic – a convenient exoneration. Even as we say we are sorry, we can wriggle out of this by telling ourselves it was not really our fault. And because we have this out – this way to pretend we were not responsible – it is easy to apologize. Which then looks duplicitous.

Obviously, this self-serving rationalization would not hold up in the court of international opinion. So to the rest of the world, Japan says, "the Japanese, a sorry lot who failed at civilian control, have decided not to possess a military." Which in turn leads some Japanese to see Article 9 as an insult and to call for its amendment. But wait a minute. What do we think of civilian control? This question has to be answered before we can even start to discuss Article 9.

And there is more than one answer to this question. It might, for example, be argued: "The war was not a failure of civilian control. From the Meiji Restoration on, all of Japan's wars were just and had the support of the vast majority of the people." I do not agree with this, but it is one position that could logically be taken. Yet it is impossible to reconcile this position with the victim mentality that says Japan suffered horribly in the war. All being fair in love and war, there is no room for whining afterward, "I didn't mean for this to happen." If you elect to go to war, your losses are your own responsibility. The people who supported the war and their successors – while they may have a responsibility to salve other people's wounds – have no right to complain about their own wounds and the horrors of war. This has to be clearly and firmly emphasized.

On the opposite extreme is the position: "We made a mess of civilian control and so we have sworn off having a military." This is also a perfectly logical position. But if you take this position, you should clearly recognize the illogic of claiming that Japan's peace Constitution is a model for the rest of the world. It is the height of conceit and projection to assume that no one else can do something just because you failed at it.

In between, there is the illogical position that the 15-year war in Asia and the Pacific was an instance of the military running amok but that Article 9 should be amended because it stigmatizes Japan as a second-class country or because Japan needs a military for policy reasons. If these people want to contend that Japan is capable of civilian control, they should first take responsibility for civilian control's past failure. And they should not join in any domestic debate about amending Article 9 until after they have been forgiven by the people who were caught up in that failure. If you were driving a car and had a horrendous accident, surely you would not be able to just unilaterally renew your own driver's license. It is the same thing. At the same time, advocates of rewriting Article 9 should work to make sure the people are more knowledgeable about military affairs and are able to bear the risks that accompany their decisions. Because "I didn't mean it to turn out that way" is no defense afterwards.

Yet as I look at the debate of late, this third position stands out. It appears at first to be a new position, but it is just an updated version of absolute pacifism in its refusal to address the issue of civilian control. In fact, it boils down to the spoiled child's, "It wasn't my fault. Why does everybody treat me like a child?" And because it resonates so comfortably with people who do not want to admit their mistakes, it is gradually becoming the new majority position. But neither the Constitution nor war should be taken so lightly. Neither should be seen as a way of compensating for an inferiority complex.

It is neither the military nor military force that erodes civilian control. Rather, it is the people's unwillingness to confront the past. Just having a "model Constitution for the rest of the world" or "a Constitution we can be proud of" is no guarantee history will not repeat itself. The real bulwark has to be civilian control by the people.

□■□ Why the Rush to Amend the Constitution?

Shibutani Hideki

Shibutani Hideki is Professor, Rikkyo (St. Paul's) University Law School.
Born in 1955. Completed doctoral coursework at University of Tokyo Graduate
School of Legal and Political Studies. Specialist in Constitutional studies. Among
his works are *Kenpou Soshou Youkenron* (Constitutional Case Law) (Shinzansha),
Kenpou e no Shoutai (Introduction to the Constitution) (Iwanami Shoten), *Nihonkoku
Kenpou no Ronjikata* (How to Talk about the Japanese Constitution) (Yuuhikaku),
Reedinguzu Gendai no Kenpou (Readings in the Constitution) (co-author, Nihon Hy-
ouronsha), *Kenpou 1 : Jinken* (The Constitution 1: Human Rights) and *Kenpou 2: Touchi*
(The Constitution 2: Governance) (co-author, both Yuuhikaku).

THERE HAS BEEN considerable discussion these last few years of amending the
Constitution. Yet I wonder if this discussion has really been grounded in the
fundamentals of the Constitution. So I would like to isolate two of the things
that have bothered me and look at them in some detail.

Amending the Constitution to stipulate more duties

One of these is the idea that the Constitution should stipulate more duties. At
present, the only duties stipulated are those of paying taxes (Article 30) and
ensuring that children receive an education (Article 26). So it may seem that
it would not be unreasonable to stipulate other duties. Yet when you think
about it, the duty to pay taxes is actually a right to not pay taxes in the absence
of any tax laws enacted by our representatives. No representation, no taxation. Likewise, the duty to educate children is one accruing to guardians and
the government and should be seen primarily as making them responsible for
ensuring that children are able to enjoy their right to receive an education.

Constitutions are actually statements of rights. To understand why this is
so, it is perhaps necessary to recall what things were like prior to the creation

of Constitutions. For a long period in human history, the people with the power (the government) at any given time flaunted their power, collected taxes, expropriated assets, conscripted the people for wars or labor, and ruthlessly crushed any who opposed them. Thus the people who conceived the idea of a Constitution thought it would be a good idea to establish protections called "human rights" within this Constitution to defend themselves against the wanton abuse of power by the government. These human rights are thus the rights naturally accruing to a human being by virtue of being a human being. And just as the right to receive an education imposed a commensurate obligation to provide an education, as seen above, rights for one side impose duties on the other side. By protecting human rights, the Constitution is constructed as a set of rules imposing obligations on the government, which could basically do whatever it wanted in pre-Constitution days. The idea that the Constitution should be amended to impose more duties and obligations on the people is thus in essential contradiction to the very essence of what the Constitution is all about.

Amending the Constitution to allow a military and to become a normal country

The other thing that has bothered me is the idea that the Constitution should be amended to provide for the Self-Defense Forces (SDF) as a military so Japan can be a normal country. We should probably start by asking what a "normal country" is and means. With Article 9, Japan has proclaimed itself a country that does not possess "land, sea, and air forces, as well as other war potential." But of course the other leading Constitutional states (meaning states whose governments are premised upon rule of law, respect for fundamental human rights, and separation of powers) such as the U.K., the U.S., and France all possess formidable militaries. Today's Japan has the SDF to provide for its own defense. So the argument is made that Article 9 should be amended to recognize the SDF as a full-out military and make Japan a "normal country."

Yet it is imperative here that we go back to the basic premises and think long and hard about what the government (state) is for. When people became aware of the need to enact a Constitution, they also concluded that the state exists to protect the lives, liberty, and property of the people. Thus Article 13 of the Japanese Constitution speaks of "the right to life, liberty, and the pursuit of happiness" as "the supreme consideration in legislation and in other governmental affairs." This is a clear statement that the prime purpose of all governmental authority (the state's very *raison d'être*) is to ensure the people lose neither life nor liberty and are able to live happily. There are some people who argue that human rights depend upon the state for their existence, but this has it backwards. It is important to be very clear about this: the state is no more than an instrument through which people pursue happiness (human rights).

Of course, it could be argued that a military is established to protect the lives of the people. But it is important to ask if militaries have ever actually been used to protect the lives of the people. In reality, militaries are typically permitted to take the lives not only of people in other countries but also the lives even of their own countrymen who oppose them, and we must never forget that this is how militaries have actually operated over the years. So long as the Constitution posits "the sanctity of human life" as the key universal right, it is wildly contradictory for it to provide for the existence of an organization used for the taking of human life. By renouncing the possession of war potential, the Constitution of Japan expresses in ultimate form the way of life of people who live freely and happily and the underlying spirit of respect for the sanctity of life.

Discerning the true intent behind talk of amending the Constitution

Given all of this, why is there any need to even talk about amending the Constitution? One possibility is that this is an effort to divert our attention from the wretched politicians we have by blaming the fact that politics is dysfunctional on the Constitution. Or it could be that those who want to amend the Constitution reject those values the Constitution holds dearest (the right to live in liberty and happiness) and want to replace them with other values. Or perhaps they want to impose the values they believe right on the rest of us by writing them into the Constitution. Or there could be some other reason.

Yet whatever the reason, it is essential each and every one of us recognize the very real danger that altering the Constitution could alter our way of life and our very lives themselves. Working from the perspectives explained above (the spirit of the Constitution), it is extremely important that we identify the real reasons behind the various arguments for amending the Constitution. As a first step, we should read the many essays in this book, keeping the Constitution's spirit in mind.

■■□ Begin by Reforming Ourselves

Sudou Genki

> Sudou Genki is a fighter/martial-artist affiliated with the Beverly Hills Ju-jitsu Club in California.
>
> Born in 1978. Started wrestling in his first year of high school. Won the Championship in the All-Japan Junior Olympics while a student at Takushoku Junior College. Went to the U.S. following graduation. Returned to Japan and made his professional debut in 1999. Won the UFC (Ultimate Fighting Championship) in July 2002 and was the first Japanese "Tap Out" winner. Active in a wide range of fields, including appearing in the film *Kyouki no Sakura* (Madness in Bloom).

TO BE PERFECTLY honest, I do not know that much about the Constitution. Of course, I know it is the Constitution, but why isn't it written in simple language that would be easy for anyone to understand? Indeed, I wonder how many people my age actually understand what the Constitution says. Laws and politics are the same. If you make them too complex and convoluted, you're just going to turn people off. In fact, I suspect the closer you get to essential truths, the simpler something looks and is.

Even so, even I know that there has been a lot of talk recently about whether or not to amend the Constitution. But I don't think rewriting the Constitution would radically transform the world we live in.

I know the Constitution is a bit fuzzy and open to different interpretations in places, and it is not even internally consistent. If you do what one place says, you're in violation of someplace else. The discussion goes on and on because each side thinks it is going to win, and it turns out that everyone is doing the right thing according to his or her own worldview.

Laws are basically an attempt to ensure fairness in public life, but the fairness has to originate in the individual. You cannot legislate morality. It would be hard to write a law that says, "Be nice to everyone." The important thing is that people be aware and mature – not that we have more laws. So I doubt if you can solve Japan's, or any of the world's, many problems with new laws alone. People have been trying that for hundreds and thousands of years, and it hasn't worked yet.

The real laws that should govern our lives do not need to be written down and spelled out. They are self-evident. For example, civilized people know better than to shoot themselves. They know it would hurt, and perhaps even be fatal. So they know not to shoot other people, either. They know it would hurt the other person – and the other person may well find a gun of his own and shoot back. But even though everyone knows this, the barbarians are in a mad race to build bigger and better guns. And so history repeats itself.

It is the same in athletics and politics. The best players are taciturn. Whether they win or lose, they don't talk about it very much. The results speak for themselves. By contrast, the second- and third-rate people spend a lot of time talking about it – regardless of the actual results, but especially if they lose, in which case they go to great lengths to explain the results away.

I suspect you could substitute "loving" for civilized and "fearful" for barbaric. When people are filled with love, they are inclusive and caring. When fear reigns, they hide, they get angry, and they attack. These two emotions – love and fear – are at the very root of human thought, language, and behavior. And it is from this basic balance that we perceive and create our environment and events. Likewise, it is from the collective orientation that we create Japan and the other nations of the world.

The important thing is not to change the Constitution and other people's thinking but to start with yourself. It is far easier to change what you think and do than it is to change other people. And if you change yourself, this is bound to influence the people around you and bring about change in the group ethic. Sure, you might not be that happy with the Constitution or with other people, but the best way to alleviate your dissatisfaction is to look at it differently. It is impossible for just one person to change the Constitution. The Constitution was created by the multitudes, and no one person exercises sufficient control to change the situation. So the only option is to change your approach.

Nothing is inherently distasteful. Rather, distastefulness stems from understanding something wrong. You want to avoid some things because you have jumped to conclusions and imposed a spin on them. If you stop imposing your interpretation on them, they stop being so repulsive. Yet you impose this or that understanding on them because of past experience and old thinking.

All creation comes from imagination. So to change it, you have to imagine new thinking and then to imbue it with new understanding.

Combat sports, which is what I do, can be very punishing. I do not know how many times I wanted to quit, but this was always because I felt ground down by the hard practice sessions or anxious about the matches. But when I turned away from that and thought instead about how I was getting stronger and growing as a person, it was suddenly less punishing and I was able to enjoy training. Looking on the bright side, I was motivated.

So I don't think we should just criticize and impose our own interpretations on things. If you criticize somebody, that person is going to criticize you. If you impose your own interpretation on something, somebody else will impose his or her interpretation on you. Far better to focus on the pleasures and joys in life and on the things that are going well. Great revolutions are born of joy.

We are all one.

□■□ Popular Sovereignty and Human Rights Had to Be Forced on Japan

Tahara Souichirou

Tahara Souichirou is a journalist and commentator.
Born in 1934. Graduated from Waseda University School of Letters, Arts and Science. Went freelance in 1977 after a career at TV Tokyo. Started *Asa made Nama
Telebi* (Live All Night Long on TV) in 1987 and *Sunday Project* in 1989. Awarded
the Galaxy 35th Anniversary Prize (the Kido Award) in 1998. Among his works
are *Nihon no Sensou: Naze Tatakai ni Fumikitta ka* (Japan's War: Why Did It Come
to This?) (Shougakkan) and *Nihon no Sensou: Watakushitachi wa Machigatte Ita ka*
(Japan's War: Were We Wrong?) (Kodansha).

THE NEW CONSTITUTION was promulgated on November 3, 1946. At the time,
I was in the sixth year in National School.

I did not read the new Constitution at the time. But I saw the newspaper
headlines, heard the radio news and commentaries, and listened to my
teachers. So I knew that the Constitution made the Emperor the symbol of
the state; that it renounced war; that it guaranteed freedom of speech, association, and assembly as well as freedom of religion; and that it proclaimed
gender equality and extended suffrage to women.

And I remember very clearly that, child though I was, I welcomed the new
Constitution. Media and teachers alike proclaimed it a wonderful Constitution – an epochal Constitution. Of course, I later came to be somewhat less
trusting of what the media and my teachers said, but…

It was, after all, just a year earlier that the same media and teachers had been
talking day in and day out exhorting us to commit "honorable suicide" and
to "die for the glory of the Emperor." Yet now they were telling us that "the
people who caused the war were animals" and "we should be willing to put

our lives on the line to prevent the outbreak of war." And in another few years they would be calling the antiwar pacifists "a bunch of commie rats."

Having endured bombings night after night, having heard of mass suicide as the honorable path less than a year earlier, and having been resigned to dying, we were delighted at Article 9's renunciation of war and saw it as delivery from death. Yet later we were forced to acknowledge that even if Japan did not cause a war, there was still the danger it could be attacked. We were forced to think once more about national security concerns.

The part of the postwar Constitution that I believe we should be willing to put our lives on the line to defend is the part about the inviolacy of the people's fundamental human rights. Article 14 provides that all of the people are equal before the law and naturally guarantees the equality of the sexes. Article 19 then states clearly that there shall be no infringement of freedom of thought or freedom of conscience, Article 20 provides freedom of religion, and Article 21 guarantees freedom of assembly and association as well as of speech, the press, and all other forms of expression.

Of course, Article 28 of the old Meiji Constitution also provided for "freedom of religious belief," with the long caveat that the people exercise such beliefs "within limits not prejudicial to peace and order, and not antagonistic to their duties as subjects." And Article 29 of that Constitution recognized that the people "enjoy the liberty of speech, writing, publication, public meetings, and association," albeit only "within the limits of law," such that all of these freedoms could disappear overnight if the law changed.

In fact, since I did not have freedom of speech and freedom of religious belief as an elementary school child, I was fully aware of the significance of the new Constitution's dropping the "within the limits of law" hedge and enshrining these as basic human rights protected by law.

We often see and hear people argue that the present Constitution was forced on Japan by the Occupation forces and that it was intended to weaken Japan and gut the Japanese spirit. While there is no disputing the fact that it was forced upon Japan by the Occupation forces, even if the Occupation had not forced a Constitution upon us, there is no way the old Constitution's claim that "the Empire of Japan shall be reigned over and governed by a line of Emperors unbroken for ages eternal" could have been maintained when Japan had surrendered unconditionally and was an occupied country. With the military disarmed and disbanded, the claims that "the Emperor has the supreme command of the Army and Navy" and "the Emperor determines the organization and peace standing of the Army and Navy" necessarily rang a bit hollow.

On the flip side, the Constitution would not have spoken of sovereignty residing in the people and would not have guaranteed fundamental human rights – not "subject to the limits of law" but directly guaranteed under the Constitution – had it not been forced upon Japan.

Public opinion may well be turning in favor of amending the Constitution. Yet, as a member of the last generation familiar with wartime conditions, I feel it is absolutely imperative that we preserve the spirit of Article 9 and the basic guarantees of fundamental human rights. Indeed, if you will pardon the somewhat righteous tone, I feel it is my mission to work for their preservation.

□■□ Don't Disenfranchse People with Disabilities

Takenaka Nami

Takenaka Nami is Chairperson, Prop Station.
Born in 1948. Graduated from Kobe Municipal Motoyama Junior High School. Inspired by the birth of her seriously handicapped daughter to begin studying education and welfare for the handicapped. Founded Prop Station in 1991 to help handicapped people find employment. Among her works are *Prop Station no Chousen* (Chikuma Shobo) (English edition *Let's Be Proud!* published by Japan Times) and *Lakkii Uuman* (Lucky Woman) (Asuka Shinsho).

MY DAUGHTER WAS born brain-damaged. My experiences raising her led me to found the nonprofit organization Prop Station in 1991 so that I could help people with disabilities lead independent lives. Our slogan is, "For a society in which people with disabilities can become taxpayers!" This phrase, which underlies our entire mission, comes from a speech given by U.S. President John F. Kennedy in 1962 in which he said he wanted to help all disabled people become taxpayers. He said he wanted the U.S. to commit to building a society in which people with disabilities can lead productive lives – can work and pay taxes – a society that will protect human rights and respect the individual. Hearing his words, I was shocked at the difference between Japan and the U.S.

I have seen the Japanese welfare system firsthand as it cared for my daughter, and it is a far cry from the one Kennedy envisioned. Japanese welfare policy seems to be, "We're giving benefits to people with disabilities, and they should leave everything to us." At first glance, this seems fine – those who are burdened with disabilities seem to be treated kindly. But clearly the hidden text is: "The handicapped are a drag on society and need to be tucked out of sight." Thus Japanese welfare policy ignores the aspirations of people with disabilities who want to earn money and become independent. People with disabilities who run up against this official attitude find it hard to keep their self-respect and go on with their lives.

The handicapped need more than just nursing care and welfare benefits. They need a program that will assist them and mainstream them back into society where they can work and play with the rest of us. It is already 40 years since this idea took hold and transformed welfare policy in the U.S. and Europe, but Japanese public opinion still exempts people with disabilities from the usual expectation that people will work and pay taxes. The result is discriminatory welfare policy that segregates people with disabilities from society.

An example: At Prop Station, we provide computer training to help people with disabilities learn skills and find work. One man took our online program from home, where he was cared for by his family, and then found work as a systems engineer. After a while, however, his situation changed and he could not be cared for at home. He entered a nursing home and wanted to work from there, but the institution refused to put a phone line in for him. Their excuse was that residents are not permitted to work. This institution for people with disabilities is actually preventing them from leading more independent lives. Even though Japan's Constitution extols respect for the individual and equality under the law, such is not the reality for those with disabilities. For them, the Constitution is merely empty words on paper.

In thinking about this idea of independence for people with disabilities, I believe we should amend Article 14's declaration of equality under the law to add, "physical or mental impairment" and "age" to the section providing that "there shall be no discrimination … because of race, creed, sex, social status or family origin." I include "age" because the Japanese population is rapidly aging and elderly people now account for a steadily increasing percentage of the total. As people age, the number with disabilities will skyrocket. Japan is being transformed, and we must respond preemptively to the changes.

I am thus devoting myself to formulating a basic law that will apply to society as a whole. The English phrase "universal design" is well known in Japan, and I think it essential we apply this idea to make life easier for people with disabilities by modifying not only the products they use and their physical surroundings but also society as a whole. We need universal design for our social structures so that everyone – not just those with disabilities – can live up to his potential in a growth-conducive environment and with the appropriate products. But enacting such a law and creating such a social system requires we first revise the Constitution – the source of all law – and bring it up to date.

Another example of the Constitution's outdatedness is the fact that it makes no mention of the victims of crime. It makes ample provision for the rights of offenders but gives no thought to the victims. We must add safeguards for these people as well. Further, Article 9 and the Self-Defense Forces look very different to us now that the increased threat of terrorism is severely stressing our international environment. Japan's commitment to pacifism is still important, but it is time for Japan to carefully examine how we can be responsible for our own defense and write a Constitution that reflects this consensus. The present Constitution was drafted by SCAP General Headquarters during the American occupation of Japan after World War II and does not, unfortunately, exemplify the will of the Japanese people. Knowing this, I can understand why some people are indifferent to it. The Constitution must be written by the Japanese people. Even if the new Constitution ends up looking like the present Constitution, it will still be a worthy achievement.

The revision process is crucial. It is essential there be full debate to bring out the best of the collective wisdom and enact our own Constitution. Indeed, this very process itself will bring the new Constitution into our hearts and awaken us to its worth.

(interview-based)

☐■☐ Re-choosing a Constitution That Respects Individuality

Ueno Chizuko

Ueno Chizuko is Professor, University of Tokyo Graduate School of Humanities and Sociology.
Born in 1948. Completed her doctoral work in sociology at Kyoto University and served as Associate Professor at Heian Jogakuin (St. Agnes) Junior College and Professor at University of Tokyo Faculty of Letters, among other things, before assuming present position. Among her many books are *Sukaato no Shita no Gekijou* (Theater Beneath the Skirt) (Kawade Shobo) and *Kindai Kazoku no Seiritsu to Shuuen* (The Rise and Fall of the Modern Family) (Iwanami Shoten). Her latest is *Sensou ga Nokoshita Mono* (The Leavings of War) (Shin'yosha).

SOME PEOPLE TALK about protecting the Constitution, some about revising the Constitution, and still others about debating the Constitution. I am interested in *choosing* the Constitution.

It is anomalous that the Constitution has not once been amended in over half a century. Almost all of the people who saw the Constitution enacted have passed away and been replaced by a new generation of Japanese. It is thus important that the current generation of Japanese go through the process of deciding what kind of a Constitution they want – even if the new Constitution ends up being the same as the present Constitution.

Admittedly, I obviously would not choose the same Constitution as that loudly espoused by the Liberal Democratic Party's Research Commission on the Constitution and other very vocal groups. My Constitution would respect the individual, which was the original objective of the current Constitution.

Public opinion becomes daily more approving of rethinking the Constitution, and revision appears inevitable. This being the case, the realistic thing to do now is to push this momentum in a direction that produces an acceptable outcome – to argue for choosing the Constitution.

How? Consider, for example, the phrase *sexual harassment*. This was originally a specialized English term that was used only by feminist scholars. As conservative males in the media over-reacted, however, it instantly became a household phrase used by one and all. The campaign against feminism became a classic illustration of the rule of unintended results. Those who want policies to deal with sexual harassment are probably saying, "You conservative geezers in the media: Thanks for raising the attention level!"

Other examples abound. Prime Minister Koizumi advocates governmental reforms that are neo-liberal in nature. One reform seeks to increase tax revenues by actively encouraging women's participation in the labor market by repealing the spouse deduction and other tax breaks that tend to limit women's working hours. Unwittingly, this action is congruent with feminist goals and promotes the individual as the tax unit for social security and taxes. Motives may be totally at odds in the world of politics, but the policy objective is often the same. Single-issue politics, as this is called, accepts this reality and works with, rather than excludes, groups with similar policy directions but tainted or conflicting motives. This is now the trend in social movements.

I would like the debate over Constitutional revision to be subject to single-issue politics. The LDP has begun to call for revision of Article 24 and its statement on individual dignity and equality of the sexes within the family. Article 24, like Article 9, has long been considered off-limits, and women's groups opposing revision are voicing their dissent. The irony is that this furor has aroused interest in Article 24, which usually receives little attention in the debate over constitutional revision, and put it on a front burner. It is very welcome that the process of choosing what kind of a Constitution we want will cause lively public discussion. Surely, it is a good thing that these issues have come to the fore.

There are three particular areas that should be the focus here: Article 1, Article 9, and Article 24. First, Article 1 should be deleted. The Constitution must return to its roots when Japan was a defeated nation and set up a republic with sovereignty invested in the people. Not only does Article 1 fog popular sovereignty; it negates the human rights of the Imperial family. It is generally accepted that international law has precedence over any one nation's constitution, and that the Imperial family has human rights under international human rights law. By discarding Article 1, we acknowledge that the Imperial family is at one with the people and that its members have the same human rights.

With respect to Article 9, for over half a century, Japan has said that it will not maintain armed forces but has maintained Self-Defense Forces capable of waging war. This is disingenuous. The government is planning to revise Article 9 to bring it in line with today's reality, but I want nothing to do with that. It is not unusual for a gap to exist between a nation's constitution and its reality. So why not ratify the postwar reality that preserved peace even with Article 9 and its inconsistencies? More specifically, we should replace the second paragraph with one clearly stating, "Military power may be maintained for self-defense, but not a single member of the military may be sent to duty outside of Japan." Once we acknowledge the Japanese capacity for self-defense, foreign troops should leave. Arms control and disarmament are our ideals for the future.

Article 24 was doubtless once a statement of individualism within marriage. Now, however, administrative law gives precedence to the couple and the household at the expense of the individual. Social security and taxation should apply to individuals as individuals. When we choose the Constitution, these distortions and contradictions must be rectified. And, in acknowledgement of gays and lesbians, Paragraph 2's talk of "the sexes" should be changed to talking of "the principals."

I have one final wish, this with respect to terminology. Wouldn't it be better if the Constitution's references to *kokumin* (Japanese citizens) were rewritten to refer to *Nihon rettou ni sumu hitobito* (the people who live in Japan)? The English version of the Japanese Constitution speaks primarily of "the people" and not specifically "the Japanese citizenry." Translating "the people" as *kokumin* was a mistake from the start, and it has resulted in all sorts of citizenship requirements being placed on the enjoyment of many rights. I think it would make much more sense in this era of global migration for the Constitution to refer to "the people who live in Japan" and not restrict "the people" to holders of Japanese nationality.

(interview-based)

□■□ Respecting the Vast Diversity of the Populace

Yamamoto Jouji

Yamamoto Jouji is a former member of the House of Representatives, currently working at a welfare facility for the disabled.

Born in 1962 in Hokkaido. First elected to the House of Representatives in 1996. Sentenced to 18 months in prison in June 2001 for misappropriating secretarial salary subsidies. Upon release, published *Gokusouki* (View from a Prison Window) (Poplar Publishing) on the charges and his time in prison.

I WONDER IF it is not more than a bit presumptuous for someone like myself – someone who has done time – to be writing about the supreme law of the land. Nevertheless, I welcome this chance to set down how I see the Constitution given my experience behind bars and what I have seen since getting out.

I was in for about 14 months. While I was there, I was assigned to help care for prisoners with disabilities. And now that I have been released, I am working at a welfare facility for the disabled and have been working to establish a welfare facility for former prisoners with disabilities.

I can never forget what one disabled prisoner told me before he was released: "Us guys with disabilities have been under sentence since birth. So it doesn't really matter where we do our time. Inside is fine. In a way, I sometimes think prison is the best place for me – that life here is better than anywhere else. People talk of normalization and making society barrier-free, but the reality still leaves a lot to be desired. Even if the physical infrastructure is made barrier-free, there are still the social barriers and the prejudice. These will never go away."

It is appalling to think he found prison – with its lack of freedoms and its lack of respect – an easier place to live. Is life on the outside really that hard for the disabled? His comment really tore me apart. At the same time, I realized how little I had done and how little I had accomplished, even though I had made welfare issues a priority when I was in the Diet. I was ashamed at the realization that all of our pretty debates and discussions of welfare policy had been just abstract theorizing.

In the Diet, I thought we were doing something for society. In prison, I realized we had just been assuaging our own guilt. With the benefit of hindsight, I realize now that the Diet makes a great show of feeling the national pulse but is actually just taking its own temperature. Just as was true of me at the time, new Diet members get co-opted, lose touch with the public, and gradually become more comfortable in the corridors of power than out among the people.

This is, of course, the same Diet where there has been a flowering of interest in the Constitution on both sides of the aisle and where the moves to amend the Constitution are taking on a greater air of plausibility. Even the Democratic Party of Japan, which I once belonged to in the Diet, has shifted from "discussing the Constitution" to "creating the Constitution." And now they appear to be in the same "Constitution reform" circle as the Liberal Democratic Party.

Given all of this, it is essential that people be on guard against the elitist assumption that might makes right and pervasive default nationalistic ideology – as well as against moves for Constitutional reform dominated by such thinking. The LDP Constitutional Reform Project Team is on record as having claimed that "respect for fundamental human rights has led to a climate of egotistical selfishness," and as wanting to strengthen the provisions mandating the duties of the people toward the state.

Personally, I believe it is only because postwar Japan had the three Constitutional pillars of popular sovereignty, pacifism, and respect for fundamental human rights that it has been able to preserve its peace and prosperity for over half a century. Yet such is not to say I flat-out reject the very idea of amending the Constitution. The present situation, in which anything that is not explicitly stated in the Constitution is left to the discretion of the politicos, seems to me very dangerous indeed. There is considerable public support for adding environmental rights, privacy protection, and other rights to the Constitution, and I have the nagging suspicion that the long taboo against discussing amending the Constitution has been a factor relegating Japan to third-world status in terms of human rights protection.

Rethinking the Constitution to ensure it is in keeping with the times is an obvious imperative in any rule-of-law country. Yet I must stand in stark opposition to any efforts to rewrite the Constitution in such a way as would impose nationalist thinking on the people or would create a state like the one envisioned by the members of the Diet. Was not democracy itself born of the desire to recognize and respect a diversity of values and views? The debate on amending the Constitution should not take place in the Diet between the government and opposition parties; a popular consensus must be sought premised upon broad debate among all of the people. If we start from this perspective, it seems clear that the bulk of the current Constitution's provisions should be preserved and the only amendments that are needed are those to remedy oversights and shortcomings.

For example, a candid look at Japanese society today reveals that there is still very considerable discrimination, and there are understandable calls for broadening and strengthening the Constitutional protections for human rights. Thus I would augment the current categories (race, creed, sex, social status, and family origin) by adding that there shall be no discrimination on the basis of age, education, wealth, family make-up, place of birth, disability, or criminal record, either. Almost all of the amendments to the U.S. Constitution – which has adopted this tack-on amendment process – deal with fundamental human rights, and Japan could do worse than to learn from America's example.

Whatever the Constitution, I hope the Diet debate on Constitutional reform will not take a condescending view of the people but will be conducted with utmost respect for them. Whatever the outcome, it is of utmost importance that the debate be such that as many people as possible can take part and make their views heard.

☐■☐ Individual Rights and the Public Good Go Together

Yamawaki Naoshi

Yamawaki Naoshi is Professor, University of Tokyo Graduate School of Arts and Sciences.

Born in 1949. Graduated from Hitotsubashi University Faculty of Economics. Specializes in social philosophy and public philosophy. Among his books are *Shin Shakai Tetsugaku Sengen* (A New Social Philosophy) (Soubunsha), which attempts to reintegrate philosophy and the social sciences; *Keizai no Ronrigaku* (Economic Ethics) (Maruzen), which proposes a new paradigm for thinking about economics ethically; and *Koukyou Tetsugaku to wa Nanika* (What Is Public Philosophy?) (Chikuma Shinsho) popularizing public philosophy.

THE ESSENTIAL DOCTRINE pervading Japan's Constitution is stated in Article 97 of Chapter X, a closing chapter that is entitled "Supreme Law." Article 97 says, "The fundamental human rights by this Constitution guaranteed to the people of Japan are fruits of the age-old struggle of man to be free; they have survived the many exacting tests for durability and are conferred upon this and future generations in trust, to be held for all time inviolate."

This statement should be seen as the ultimate reaffirmation of the importance of the specifics in Articles 10 through 40 of Chapter III: Rights and Duties of the People. We must never lose sight of Articles 12 and 13's assertions: "The freedoms and rights guaranteed to the people by this Constitution shall be maintained by *the constant endeavor of the people*, who shall refrain from any abuse of these freedoms and rights and shall always be responsible for utilizing them for *the public welfare*" and "All of the people shall be respected as individuals. Their right to life, liberty, and the pursuit of happiness shall, to the extent that it does not interfere with *the public welfare*, be the supreme consideration in legislation and in other governmental affairs." (Emphasis added)

Especially noteworthy is that Articles 12 and 13 clearly state that fundamental individual rights cannot be separated from "the endeavor of the people" and "the public welfare." Despite this, there has not been much philosophically meaningful discussion of this issue. As an unfortunate consequence, some politicians and media commentators have recently put forth the absurd contention that postwar Japan has placed too much emphasis on individual dignity and has neglected the idea of community. And then they go on from there to say the Fundamental Law of Education should be amended – it seems to me for the worse.

Responding to this alarming situation, I would argue that individual rights and the public good are not opposing and contradictory doctrines but are in fact complementary concepts. What we need is the public philosophy of *kasshi kaikou*, or "animating the private and opening the public," where individual rights and the public good thrive together.

"Animating the private and opening the public" is the opposite of both *messhi houkou*, which advocates the sacrifice of personal interests in order to serve the public, and *mekkou houshi*, in which only the personal life is enjoyed and the public good is neglected. *Kasshi kaikou* thinking empowers the individual and brings public-spiritedness to bloom, thereby opening the government to the public.

Yet this "public realm" concept is fundamentally different from the world of government and authorities. According to the great 20th-century thinker Hannah Arendt, the public realm can only be created through communication among people having both similarities and differences and must be as open as possible. The public realm does not originate from the orders of government authorities. Together, "animating the private and opening the public" and "the public realm," are ways of giving shape to the "public good" concept. Such thinking is critical for Japan today.

Sacrificing one's individual interests to the national community was praised as a virtue in the years leading up to and during World War II. This idea persists even in postwar Japan in the form of the organization man who sacrifices himself and his family for the company. Today, the corporation has replaced the state as the embodiment of community, but the spirit of giving priority to the greater organizational interest continues. The frequency of *karoushi* (death from overwork) and suicide due to work-related stress speaks to this point. By contrast, valuing one's personal interests at the expense of the public interest implies a lifestyle devoid of any sense of the public, as illustrated by the recluse who retreats into his own private world and the person who is consumed by private greed. In a world permeated with such attitudes on both sides, it is not surprising that *individual rights* and *the public good* are seen in contradiction to each other. However, the concept of "animating the private and opening the public" stands in opposition to both the idea that individual interests should be sacrificed for the sake of the community and the idea that community interests are irrelevant in the quest for individual gratification. This doctrine values the modern idea of human rights as well as the civic virtue of feeling responsible for both oneself and others. It argues the complementary nature of *individual rights* and *the public good.*

This idea also provides the logical link joining Articles 25, 29, and 30. Paragraph 1 of Article 25 discusses the right to a decent standard of living ("All people shall have the right to maintain the minimum standards of wholesome and cultured living"); Paragraph 2 of Article 29 property rights ("Property rights shall be defined by law, in conformity with the public welfare"); and Article 30 the payment of taxes ("The people shall be liable to taxation as provided by law"). It is the philosophy of individual rights within the public well-being framework that makes these articles complementary.

Nor is that all. The public philosophy of "animating the private and opening the public" means that the "peace for all time" mentioned in the Preamble and in Article 9 is not a passive concept but asserts peace as an active and positive idea based on communication with the people. Spinoza rejected the view of peace as merely the absence of war and defined it as "virtue that emanates from the power of the soul." He believed that peace could be achieved only through "cooperation based on endeavor and spiritual power" – which means peace is attainable. A citizenry that aspires sincerely to an international peace based on justice and order and that forever renounces war and the use of force must use this philosophy to send the message of the peace Constitution to the world at large.

☐■☐ Full of Ambiguity and Widely Ignored

Yasuda Yoshihiro

Yasuda Yoshihiro is a lawyer.

Born in 1947. Graduated from Hitotsubashi University. Is a central presence in the movement to abolish the death penalty. Was the lead defense lawyer in a number of celebrated capital cases, including the person accused of setting fire to a crowded bus in Shinjuku (Tokyo) and the Tsukasa-chan kidnapping case in Yamanashi (both 1980). In 1998, while head of the defense team for Aum Shinrikyou guru Asahara Shoukou, was arrested and indicted on charges of obstruction of compulsory seizure. Found not guilty after 10 months incarceration. Was defended by a 1,200-strong team of lawyers.

I WAS DEEPLY moved when I first read the Constitution. But now when I reread it, I don't get the same feeling at all. To be frank, the contents and the text of the Preamble seem absurd.

The Preamble states that sovereign power rests with the people. But read the Constitution itself and you'll find at the beginning that Article 1 establishes the Imperial system – an absolute contradiction of the idea of popular sovereignty. The Preamble also extols absolute pacifism, but what would we do if Japan were actually invaded? Article 9 renounces war and the possession of war potential, but would we use military force to defend ourselves or would we stick to nonviolence even if it meant dying? It's irresponsible that the constitutional guidelines aren't clear.

The same pattern runs throughout the guarantee of fundamental human rights. Article 11 says: "The people shall not be prevented from enjoying any of the fundamental human rights. These fundamental human rights guaranteed to the people by this Constitution shall be conferred upon the people of this and future generations as eternal and inviolate rights." We must never transgress fundamental human rights. But Articles 12 and 13 immediately state that these rights are only guaranteed when they are consistent with the overarching needs of the public. This bait and switch enrages me.

The death penalty is the same. Article 36 absolutely forbids torture and cruel punishment, but Article 31 accepts capital punishment, stating simply that no person shall be deprived of life except according to procedure established by law. Totally inconsistent!

When all is said and done, no law is so ignored as our Constitution. How could it be otherwise when the entire Constitution is ambiguous and riddled with contradictions? Since Japan espouses popular sovereignty, the public should at least have the opportunity to select or dismiss the prime minister, important government officials, judges, public prosecutors, police officials, and other public servants. Yet there are no provisions for this in the Constitution.

I can point out any number of instances in which the Constitution has not been upheld, but I will limit myself to Articles 31 through 40, which stipulate the protection of human rights in the criminal justice system. As I mentioned earlier, Article 31 states that no person shall be deprived of life except according to procedure established by law. However, there is no legal provision for the administration of the death penalty, which is traditionally left up to prison officials. Article 32 says no person shall be denied the right of access to the courts, but we, the people, are not at liberty to choose the judges. Articles 33 and 35 state that no person shall be arrested without a court warrant unless he is caught while committing a crime, and that no searches and seizures are permissible without a search warrant. But in fact the courts almost never deny a request for such a warrant, leaving the police and prosecutors free to do as they please. Recently, the Deposit Insurance Corporation of Japan and the Public Security Intelligence Agency have been given the authority to conduct such actions without warrants. Such authority goes far beyond their jurisdictions.

Article 34 stipulates that people may not be arrested or detained without the right to legal counsel. Nonetheless, there is no similar protection in cases of imprisonment to serve a sentence or of involuntary admission into a mental institution. Article 36 forbids torture and cruel punishment. But long hours of interrogation by police and prosecutors behind closed doors fit the definition of torture, while harsh prison conditions and brutal treatment are cruel punishment indeed. Article 37 gives the accused the right to have a fair trial, summon witnesses, and request legal counsel. However, the accused can neither select nor dismiss his court-appointed lawyer; the police and prosecution control all the evidence and do not disclose any that is favorable to the accused; and the small number of defense witnesses pales in comparison to the number the public prosecutor can summon.

Article 38 speaks out against forced confessions and states that such confessions may not be used as evidence. Here, too, the reality is wildly different. Arrest and detention are widely used to obtain confessions, and torture and threats are routine. Not only do the courts accept such confessions; they aggressively accept them as decisive evidence of guilt. The reality of criminal justice is that once someone gives in to torture and confesses, he is inevitably found guilty. Article 39 says that no person shall be held criminally liable for an act of which he has been acquitted. However, when the verdict is "not guilty," the prosecution is still allowed to appeal to higher courts in hopes of obtaining a conviction. Article 40 says that any person may sue for criminal indemnity when acquitted after arrest or detention. His compensation, however, is a mere ¥10,000 or so per day. Thus, the hard fact is that in the realm of criminal justice, as elsewhere, Japan does not abide by its Constitution.

Japan invaded so many countries and took so many lives during World War II. Why is it that we were unable to learn from those actions and create a constitution that would prevent future killing and would protect other peoples' civil rights? It is essential we create a decent constitution and live up to it.

□■□ Legal Work-arounds Are No Substitute

Yoshikuni Ichirou

Yoshikuni Ichirou is a former top bureaucrat.

Born in 1916. Graduated from Tokyo Imperial University Faculty of Law in 1940 and went to work for the Ministry of Commerce and Industry. Appointed Director-General of the Cabinet Legislation Bureau in 1972. Since resigning that post, has served in a variety of capacities including Japan Regional Development Corporation President, Nippon Telegraph and Telephone (NTT) Advisor, Japan Professional Baseball Commissioner, Japan Telecommunication Industries Federation Chairman, and Nippon Telegraph and Telephone (NTT) Special Advisor. Awarded Grand Cordon of the Order of the Sacred Treasure in 1988 and Grand Cordon of the Order of the Rising Sun in 1995.

I GAVE THE Constitution serious study when I was Cabinet Legislation Bureau Director-General under Prime Ministers Tanaka (Kakuei) and Miki (Takeo). And I had long and numerous discussions with many politicians during that period. Yet almost all of these discussions were about the interpretation of Article 9 and Japan's right of individual self-defense.

Because the government and the ruling party were so focused on interpreting the Constitution to allow the right of individual self-defense, there was inadequate discussion of the right of collective self-defense. Yet with the changes in the international situation since the collapse of Cold War structures – including the Gulf War, the Iraq War, and other developments – the right of collective self-defense has become a more important issue over the last decade or so.

Very honestly, the traditional right of individual self-defense cannot possibly be stretched to encompass the current cooperation with the U.S., the dispatch of Self-Defense Forces overseas, and the rest. The many special measures laws that exist bear witness to this impossibility.

It is now more than half a century since the Constitution was promulgated, but it has not once been amended. Yet the Constitution is not writ in stone for all time. You can look all over the world for countries that have not amended their Constitutions, and you will likely find just Japan and the Principality of Monaco. So isn't it about time the Japanese Constitution was amended to bring it into line with Japan's altered circumstances?

Article 9 heads the list of things that need to be changed. Even if Paragraph 1 is left unchanged, Paragraph 2 should be deleted and a paragraph inserted in its stead bringing the Constitution into line with reality by providing that Japan can exercise the right of collective defense in the same way as any other normal country can. Under the UN Charter, there is only one concept of the right of self-defense, and exercising this right is only natural when a country's security is threatened. Yet because of the constraints embedded in Article 9, Japan divides this into a right of individual self-defense and a right of collective self-defense.

In personal terms, it is unreasonable that an individual would only be allowed to act in defense of his or her own person. When a member of your family, a friend, or someone else you are close to is in danger, it is only human nature to want to do something to protect that person. The same is true of states, and there is no justification for separating the right of individual self-defense and the right of collective self-defense.

While we are amending the Constitution, it would also be a good idea to rewrite the Preamble. The draft for the Preamble is said to have been written by (Government Section Deputy Director Colonel Charles L.) Kades at the Supreme Commander for Allied Powers (SCAP) Headquarters, but the Japanese is stilted and obviously a translation. It lacks dignity in Japanese, and it is not clear. Worse, there are parts that appear to be apologizing to the Allied powers. What we need is a lofty statement in literary Japanese setting forth the nature of the Japanese state and then elucidating the three principles of respect for basic human rights, popular sovereignty, and pacifism.

Another part that needs amending is that on the position of the Emperor. This needs to be clarified. In discussions to date, it has not been clear whether the Emperor is the head of state or not. Yet the fact that he receives ambassadors and ministers posted to Japan and receives 21-gun salutes when visiting other countries, among other things, makes it clear that he is in fact the head of state. Consideration should thus be given to providing explicit statement that he is the head of state and that Japan is a Constitutional monarchy.

We also need to rewrite the provisions on the rights of the people. Some articles talk of "the Japanese people" and some of "all of the people." It is not clear if this latter just means all of the people with Japanese nationality or if it includes non-Japanese as well. It would be good to make the wording consistent and to make it clear who is to enjoy these rights.

Likewise, there are a number of articles such as that on detention that can be adequately covered under the provisions of the Code of Criminal Procedure. And on the other side of the coin, there is nothing at all on the rights of victims, so it would be good to think about including new provisions on the rights of the victims of criminal acts. Getting these things organized and making the provisions on the rights of the people easier to understand, the Constitution should be amended to produce a clear document.

Looking at the judiciary, I do not think the new Constitutional Court that is being talked about should be created, given the likelihood of a wanton spate of frivolous suits seeking Constitutional judgments. This should continue to be dealt with as at present.

Yet there is one thing that needs to be looked at even before any of this, and that is the issue of procedures for amending the Constitution. As it now stands, amending the Constitution requires a concurring vote of two-thirds or more of all the members of each House and the affirmative vote of a majority of all votes cast in a referendum. This is an abnormally high bar, and it is one of the reasons the Japanese Constitution is called a rigid Constitution – so much so that some people argue it makes the Constitution amendment-proof.

Previous administrations have, in fact, readied legislation setting out specific procedures for a national referendum and the other things needed to amend the Constitution, but it was always felt that amendment would be too difficult and these attempts were always shelved. The Constitution cannot be amended overnight. The people need to fully debate the issues in advance, meaning that the amount of time needed should be measured in decades. But while the issues involved are being fully debated, work should also begin on amendments that build a little more flexibility into the process of amending the Constitution.

(interview-based)

□■□ Some Japanese Views

Organizations

□ ■ □ A New Constitution for a New Era

Liberal Democratic Party

RULE-OF-LAW COUNTRIES uphold their Constitutions as the supreme law of the land. The United States and other countries with written Constitutions have thus sought to amend their Constitutions from time to time in keeping with their historical circumstances. By contrast, Japan has kept its Constitution unchanged as it was handed down by the foreign Occupation forces and has sought to respond to the changing times and circumstances with creative interpretations and re-interpretations of this basic law by the government. Yet there are limits to what can be done with interpretation and re-interpretation alone. This is especially true in the area of national security, which underlies our peace and prosperity, and it is thus imperative that the people, who hold the sovereign power to establish the Constitution, and their representatives in the Diet join together to take a hard look at Japan's circumstances and establish a new Constitution as befits this new era.

The three core principles in the Constitution – popular sovereignty, pacifism, and respect for fundamental human rights – have been wholeheartedly accepted by the people and have contributed importantly to Japan's postwar peace and recovery. This is something all of us can and should appreciate. These basic principles – these universal values – should be upheld and developed in the new Constitution as follows.

First, seeking to protect the lives and property of Japanese citizens in times of emergency, the new Constitution should have explicit provision for the possession of war potential for self-defense, and there should also be an explicit provision enabling Japan to contribute unstintingly to international peace in protecting the lives and property of people worldwide. In laying down the rules for such international contributions, it is essential that the most careful study be given to incorporating the traditional Japanese values of respect for harmony and reverence for life, as well as the lessons learned from history and our determination to never again repeat our horrific wartime experience. It is also essential we clearly delineate those areas in which Japan can make a direct contribution and those areas in which our contribution must necessarily be more limited.

Second, the new Constitution should be written in easy-to-understand and beautiful Japanese depicting the kind of society and state we want for the future. In addition, it should contain explicit provision for environmental rights, the right to know, privacy, and other new rights; and it should, consistent with the desire to ensure respect for the individual, position family and community as basic repositories of happiness that sustain society. Moreover, it should reflect our pride in Japanese history, traditions, culture, and more, and should be a Constitution that can represent Japan and Japanese society to all of the world.

Third, thought needs to be given to the structure of our political institutions, including the bicameral Diet and the relationship between the Diet and the Cabinet, in order to ensure that Japan is able to respond to changes in Japan and worldwide with quick, appropriate political leadership. It would also be well to consider establishing a Constitutional Court to ensure that the values espoused in the Constitution are realized. It will also be necessary to incorporate consideration of new modalities of local government, including the creation of "regional states," and the basic principles for their implementation (e.g., the principle of self-determination and self-responsibility and the principle of complementarity).

Finally, the process of amending the Constitution will entail the first national referendum in Japanese history, and the creation of this Constitution will thus be immensely significant. Along with working to promptly enact the necessary national referendum law for amending the Constitution, greater efforts must be made to win the wholehearted understanding and support of all of the people.

Yasuoka Okiharu
(Chairman, Research Commission on the Constitution)

□■□ A Constitution for Building a New Society

Democratic Party of Japan

HAVING ESTABLISHED ITS Constitution Research Committee in 1999, the Democratic Party of Japan has been discussing the issues involved in an effort to establish a living Constitution appropriate to our changing times. At present, the government's practice of revising the Constitution through interpretations and re-interpretations has ended up sapping the life out of the Constitution and making it just so much empty rhetoric, with the result that public faith in the Constitution has been seriously eroded. If we are to reverse this trend and establish Constitution-based politics, it is essential we have a creative discussion about what kind of a Constitution would be best for this new century.

For many years now, Japan has had a very centralized system in which the bureaucrats have wide discretion to determine policy. Indeed, many observers have said this government by bureaucratic fiat has undermined the very principle of rule of law. Even worse, our America-first foreign policy has meant that the Self-Defense Forces have been sent overseas repeatedly with no regard for the rules; the reality is that the Security Treaty, not the Constitution, seems to be the supreme law of the land.

The Constitutional revisions that the DPJ advocates are primarily intended to escape the clutches of today's dangerous reality and re-establish Constitutional government – to create a society in which rule of law is the norm. This is Constitutional creation in the proactive sense of thinking about what kind of a Constitution we need for the future rather than forever looking back at the past.

Given this approach, the DPJ Constitution Research Committee announced its interim proposals in June 2004. Among the main proposals were:

First, the changes and new values accompanying globalization and the readier availability of information mean we need a dilution of state sovereignty and more shared sovereignty such as is seen in Europe. We also need to be paying more attention to living at peace with our Asian neighbors.

Second, we need a clear statement of the Prime Minister's executive powers and greater appointive power, need to institute national referenda, need to establish a Constitutional Court and Executive Oversight Board, and need to build in some other fundamental reforms to enhance popular sovereignty and ensure that government is politics-driven.

Third, the need to create a more decentralized society means we need to establish the principle that the national government and local governments are complementary equals, ensure that local governments have the independent authority to enact laws and to tax, and promote local government diversity grounded in citizen initiative.

Fourth, the Constitution should make explicit provision for the rights of privacy and reputation, the right to know, environmental rights, and the right of self-determination, for example, and should include provisions establishing human rights commissions and ombudsmen boards as independent agencies to establish new rights and guarantee all human rights.

Fifth, aghast at the way the rules against sending the SDF overseas have been trampled and ignored, we would allow participation in UN collective security operations to secure true peace on the basis of international cooperation and would clearly establish a limited right of self-defense and *only* self-defense.

With these reforms, we seek to break free of the centralized-control-but-minimal-information-sharing pattern that pervades Japanese politics and government and to achieve true self-government in which the people have both the authority and the responsibility to make their own decisions. As such, we seek to create a society of citizen independence and mutuality within the community and of cooperation and symbiosis in Asia as a whole.

Sengoku Yoshito
(Chair, Constitution Research Committee)

◻◼◻ Adding to the Constitution to Save It

Komei Party

EVER SINCE ITS founding in 1964, the Komei Party has positioned itself as a party protecting the Constitution and defending the three core Constitutional principles of fundamental human rights, popular sovereignty, and pacifism. That stance remains unchanged even today.

Yet it would be wrong to see this Constitution as something set in stone, and we believe it is essential we have the courage to amend it so as to strengthen these three core principles in keeping with the times. Thus it is that our position has evolved to one of advocating Constitutional enhancements.

The November 2002 National Convention affirmed that the Constitution's three core principles are universal principles and that our basic policy is one of firmly upholding Article 9. At the same time, responsive to the changing times, it was decided to make an effort to reach an intra-party consensus on adding new rights such as environmental rights and privacy rights, clarifying the devolution of authority to local governments, and effecting some other enhancements. Our stance is one of adding to and augmenting the Constitution, and it is in this spirit that we have held discussions with people across the political spectrum, putting everything on the table. We expect to be able to make our position on these issues clear in the fall of 2004.

On the issue of Article 9 and the desire for lasting peace, we obviously want to keep Paragraph 1 with its renunciation of war as it is. Recognizing that Paragraph 2's statement that Japan will not possess war potential should not be interpreted as meaning Japan will not even maintain the ability to defend itself, we would add wording to that effect in a new Paragraph 3 to clarify the meaning of Paragraph 2. This is another instance in which the Constitution can usefully be augmented.

Yet even though we would add a provision recognizing the Self-Defense Forces' existence, the consensus is that it is still important to be very clear that the SDF are purely for defense and will never be sent overseas. If they are to be made available for peacekeeping operations and other forms of international cooperation, this should be clearly spelled out in the Preamble or in a new provision added for this purpose.

In all of this, the intent is to avoid undermining Article 9's international significance while still respecting to the utmost the initiatives taken by the Japanese government based upon its interpretation of Article 9 to date. Realizing the ramifications of a total rewriting of Article 9, this is an effort to augment Article 9 in acknowledgement of what it has come to mean. That said, it has also been suggested that there is no need to tamper with Article 9 at all and that the same effect can be achieved by putting these provisions in a basic law on national security.

If it proves difficult to get agreement on this point, it might make sense, as some people have suggested, to start with those items on which there is broad multi-party agreement, such as environmental rights and privacy rights, and then to work gradually to augment the Constitution from there.

Akamatsu Masao
(Director, House of Representatives
Research Commission on the Constitution)

☐■☐ Keeping All of the Constitution's Provisions for 21st-century Nation-building

Japanese Communist Party

THE JAPANESE CONSTITUTION has a number of outstanding features that anticipated the tide of history.

One, of course, is Article 9 with its declaration that Japan will neither possess war potential nor wage war. Indicative of the powerful attraction this has for the rest of the international community, it was proposed at the United Nations 2000 Millennium Forum that all countries adopt similar legislation and adhere to the principle of non-use of force. Indeed, the world hopes Japan will engage in diplomacy for peace grounded in Article 9.

Even though the government has drafted and passed an array of new legislation to justify sending the Self-Defense Forces overseas, all of this legislation has had to be premised upon the assumption that the SDF will not engage in hostilities overseas – this because Article 9 acts as a brake and keeps Japan from going down that slippery slope. Thus the primary aim of those making the most noise in favor of Constitutional reform is to eliminate this constraint and transform Japan into a country that can join the U.S. in waging war around the globe. This is what Deputy Secretary of State Richard Armitage meant when he said Article 9 is an obstacle to the smooth functioning of the U.S.–Japan alliance.

We are opposed to these efforts to turn Japan into a war-making country. Article 9 was founded on the sacrifices of millions and on remorse at Japan's war of aggression, and it is something we can take pride in before all the world. Steadfastly preserving and adhering to Article 9 is the best way to develop friendly relations with the other peoples of Asia and worldwide.

Yet Article 9 is not the Constitution's only outstanding feature, and it is also worth mentioning Article 25's clear statement of the right to life. Of all the

Summit countries, only Italy and Japan have Constitutions that declare that the people have a right to maintain the minimum standards of wholesome and cultured living and that the government has a responsibility to promote and extend social welfare. With the heightening anxiety over pensions and life in general, it is essential that these rights be realized across the board.

Similarly, Articles 14 and 24 provide for gender equality. There has been considerable progress in this direction worldwide, including the adoption of the Convention on the Elimination of All Forms of Discrimination Against Women in 1979, but the Constitution is already fully able to accommodate the progress on this important issue. The important thing now is to bring conditions in Japan into line with this Constitutional principle, including correcting the wage disparity that makes women's wages only about half of men's.

There are some people who argue that environmental rights and privacy rights have to be added to the Constitution. Yet it is fully possible to achieve these rights within the context of the fundamental human rights guaranteed by the current Constitution.

The real need is not to rewrite the Constitution. It is to get the government to give greater expression to the values that are already there. The real need is to preserve all of the Constitution's provisions and ensure that the outstanding provisions on peace, human rights, and democracy are the basis for nation-building in the 21st century.

□■□ Their Ulterior Motives

Social Democratic Party

THE SOCIAL DEMOCRATIC PARTY is determined to preserve the Constitution unchanged. As such, we refuse to accept the debasement of the Constitution – especially the gutting of Article 9.

The SDP believes that the universal principles embodied in the Constitution – popular sovereignty, pacifism, and fundamental human rights – can serve as a model for all mankind. Those who advocate revising the Constitution say it is impossible for Japan to contribute to the international community with the present Constitution the way it is. The SDP has no problem with the idea of contributing to the international community, yet we do not see Japan's international contribution in military terms. Rather, we contend that Japan should contribute in non-military ways – that Japan should contribute in the medical, educational, environmental, and other areas as epitomized by relief efforts in the wake of natural disasters and efforts to boost social development in the less-developed countries. Thanks to Article 9, Japan has not killed a single person overseas for the last 59 years. This is an international contribution we can be proud of.

The Preamble to the Constitution declares, "We recognize that all peoples of the world have the right to live in peace, free from fear and want." Protective of the Constitution, the SDP contends that this right to live in peace – this right of peaceful existence – is the most fundamental of human rights. Given that it is civilian populations who have been the main victims of modern warfare, we renounce war and believe maintaining the peace is of overriding importance.

One of the features characterizing our defense of the Constitution is the importance we place on Article 13's respect for individuals and their right to the pursuit of happiness. While advocates of amending the Constitution have recently taken to emphasizing the state over the individual – the public over the private – we take the opposite position. In fact, the SDP is working to create a society in which each and every person is respected as an individual and people live together acknowledging each other's strengths.

The advocates of amending the Constitution cite the supposed need to add such "new rights" as the right to know, the right to privacy, and environmental rights. Yet these rights can be fully recognized by the courts based upon Articles 13 and 25. Not only is there no need to amend the Constitution; it would be better to spend that energy on developing the various basic laws and specific laws and regulations that are appropriate in this area.

The real aim of those advocating Constitutional revision is to delete Paragraph 2 of Article 9, establish the Self-Defense Forces as a formal military force, and open the way to having the SDF take part in collective self-defense and hostilities. We will not allow this rewriting of Article 9. Rather, we believe that preserving the peace is the best way for Japan to occupy an honored place in the international society. Thus the SDP is determined, from its Constitution-protective position, to work to break the political stalemate, improve conditions so society more closely approximates the Constitution's ideals, and achieve a society of peace, freedom, equality, and co-existence.

□■□ Amending the Constitution for Independent Individuals and an Independent State

Keizai Doyukai

THE MAIN PROBLEM with the Japanese Constitution is that the people did not have the chance to create this Constitution of their own free will, to amend it if and as necessary, and hence to exercise this most important aspect of popular sovereignty. The people have not had any meaningful discussion of such essential issues as what the Constitution should say and what forms the state should take and have left the government to finesse everything with workarounds. As a result, the more important an issue is to the essential state, the less relevant the Constitution is to actual policy.

Keizai Doyukai's Discussion Group on Constitutional Issues sent a questionnaire out to Keizai Doyukai members in 2002. Over 90% of the respondents indicated that they thought the Constitution needs to be amended. Conditions both within Japanese society and in the international community are now radically different from what they were when the Constitution was adopted, as is the people's thinking about the state. Thus it is essential that there be a national debate on the Constitution and that the Constitution state clearly what kind of state we want Japan to be and how we want to take part in the international community.

1. Revising the Constitution for independent individuals and an independent state

Right after the war, there was inadequate understanding and awareness of the relationship between the individual and the state, and all kinds of barriers were put in the way of democracy's sound development for all manner of reasons. Likewise, with the diversification of popular values sparked by, *inter alia*, rapid globalization and the information revolution, it is imperative that we establish a shared popular awareness of what kind of a state we want and the relationship between the state and the individual, as well as that we create a social order grounded in independent individuals.

With the end of the Cold War and the increasing opacity in the international situation, we need more discussion of what national interests and values Japan should defend, the systems that are needed for this and how they can be structured, and what responsibilities each of us should bear.

2. Specific points for discussion

PREAMBLE: There should be some framing of Japan's national identity and the initiatives it can take in building world peace.

THE EMPEROR AS SYMBOL: While retaining the Emperor as symbol, we need to consider such issues as the relationship between the Emperor's position and popular sovereignty.

FOREIGN POLICY AND NATIONAL SECURITY: Efforts need to be made to change the government's position on collective self-defense, create a legal framework enabling Japan to respond in times of emergency, and put in place a structure for collecting and analyzing critical information for crisis management. Foreign policy and national security strategy need to be formulated and executed in full awareness of diplomatic, economic, humanitarian, human rights, energy, and other considerations.

POPULAR RIGHTS AND RESPONSIBILITIES AND THE PUBLIC WELFARE: The concept of the public welfare needs to be clearly established.

GOVERNING INSTITUTIONS: The disparity between the Constitution and reality needs to be rectified and this reflected in all laws and regulations, as well as in their implementation.

MAKING THE CONSTITUTION COME ALIVE: A law needs to be drawn up and enacted soon providing for a national referendum on amending the Constitution, and a Constitutional Court should also be established.

3. In summary

While rethinking the kind of state we want and incorporating these conclusions into the Constitutional debate will take quite a bit of time, those reforms that can be implemented within the present Constitutional framework should be pursued with all due haste even as Constitutional revision is being debated.

(Keizai Doyukai Secretariat)

■□ A Proposal in the National Interest

Japan Chamber of Commerce and Industry

THE JAPAN AND Tokyo Chambers of Commerce and Industry have, under Chairman Yamaguchi Nobuo's leadership, established a Discussion Forum on Constitutional Issues chaired by (Yokohama Chamber of Commerce and Industry chair) Takanashi Masayoshi and begun their own deliberations of Constitutional issues. This is a 12-member Forum including not only businesspeople but also academics and other experts.

The first meeting, held on July 6, 2004, heard from invited speaker Nakayama Tarou, chair of the House of Representatives' Research Commission on the Constitution, on the state of discussions in the Diet. This was followed by a lively exchange of views both with Nakayama and among Forum members.

Wrap-up planned for May 2005

We see the Constitution as an issue that affects small business and all of the people. Accordingly, the Forum is moving to summarize its studies and submit suggestions on those issues of special concern to the Chambers as broad-based community organizations. An interim report is expected to be issued in October 2004 and the final set of recommendations in May 2005. Looking ahead, we intend to devote further study to:

PREAMBLE: E.g., including a clear statement of distinctively Japanese values rooted in our history, traditions, and culture.

NATIONAL SECURITY: E.g., acknowledging the need for Japan, as a global player, to share responsibility for its own and other countries' security and providing for the possession of defense capability and war potential.

RIGHTS AND RESPONSIBILITIES: E.g., elucidating the relationship between the public weal and respect for human rights and including such new rights as the right to privacy and environmental rights.

EDUCATION: E.g., noting both the rights and obligations involved and highlighting the importance of the home.

LOCAL GOVERNMENT: E.g., promoting devolution, including a clear statement of the basic thinking and concept of local empowerment, and considering a regional-state structure.

□■□ Guaranteeing the Right to Quality Medical Care

Japan Medical Association

AS PHYSICIANS RESPONSIBLE for protecting the health and lives of the people, we would especially emphasize three points with regard to the Constitution: (1) the need for unqualified adherence to a philosophy of respect for life, (2) the need to redefine the right to life as guaranteed by the Constitution, and (3) the need for thoroughgoing human rights education.

With its peace Constitution adopted in the wake of that devastating war, Japan managed to become a nation of peace where no lives have been lost to the terrible ravages of war. Yet even as we have become comfortable with this situation, the future has been cast in doubt. The headline-making incidents in which Japanese have been taken hostage overseas and the threat of domestic terrorism aside, over 30,000 Japanese commit suicide every year, there has recently been an increase in violent crime, often involving the taking of innocent lives, and life seems to have been extraordinarily cheapened. Similarly, the advances in assisted reproductive technology and regenerative medicine have highlighted the imperative that all cells, membranes, organs, and other bodily parts be accorded the utmost respect as derived from the human body. Now more than ever, it is essential people realize the irreplaceable value of human life and incorporate this ideal into the Constitution as the fundamental law of the land.

The right to life enshrined in Article 25 is a crucial pillar supporting the universal health insurance that underlies Japanese medical care. This should continue to be maintained. And since the state obviously has a duty to draw up and implement the total range of social welfare policies based upon Article 25, it is essential that we, as medical professionals, be ever-aware and constantly reexamine these plans and policies to ensure they are appropriate and deserving of the people's support. Just as expectations for quality of life naturally rise with socioeconomic development, so do expectations of medical care. This means that the right to medical care must be understood and even rewritten in this context as the right to quality medical care and peace of mind. And in moving from right to reality, it is essential we ensure that everyone has access to medical care under the universal health insurance scheme, improve the quality of the medical care that is available, and work to improve and enhance the various systems involved to ensure that people have the safe, trusted care they need. It is crucial that the medical profession and the government cooperate to achieve these aims.

Medical advances have vastly improved the quality of care and brought new hope to people suffering injury or ailment, but medicine now also has the potential to wreak new tragedy if it is misused. For example, the rise of genetic testing makes it possible to map a person's physical traits more closely and even to predict disposition to certain afflictions. Yet at the same time, there is the danger that this genetic information could be used for non-research, non-medical ends such as insurance screening and hiring selection, thereby making it a tool for discrimination. It is thus essential broad-based human rights education be undertaken throughout society so as to achieve a society free of bias and discrimination where all are aware of how this technology can best be used to provide the very best medical care possible.

☐■☐ Looking for Government
   that Will Live the Constitution

Shufuren

FOUNDED IN 1948, Shufuren has long worked in the context of the realization that peace is prerequisite to safety and peace of mind. Indeed, our movement grew out of the wasteland that was Japan in the war's aftermath. Other guiding principles have been equally obvious and easy to understand, including the idea that rotten government means rotten lives and that housewives need to have a bigger voice in politics. Yet the bulk of our activity over the last half-century-plus has been driven by the desire to create a society free of war – a society of peace.

We have also sought to improve people's lives in other ways, including campaigning against defective products and misleading labels, protesting unwarranted price hikes, striving to have consumer interests reflected in policy decision-making, and even campaigning for the creation of a Ministry of Consumer Affairs. In 1950, we were first in Japan to begin product testing by actual consumers, as part of our focus on product safety, quality, and value.

In 1957, we adopted a consumer manifesto proudly declaring consumer sovereignty and held the first national congress bringing together consumer organizations and labor unions. We have evolved over the years from a consumer movement fighting to protect our lives and livelihoods to a movement in which sovereign consumers fight to establish consumer rights.

Japan's peace Constitution has been the bedrock for all we do. The 2004 Annual General Meeting adopted a 55th anniversary manifesto of policy recommendations and action plans, the first of which was a call to uphold the peace Constitution with pride and preserve peace. We are also working to expand the network of organizations working for peace and to get the government to live the Constitution. This includes taking part in the annual peace picnic held outside the *Daigo Fukuryuu Maru* exhibition hall, participating in the international women for peace program as part of the International Year of Women, and joining hands with a wide range of other progressive citizen organizations to oppose sending the Self-Defense Forces to Iraq. In May 2004, we took part in the Constitution Commemoration Congress and adopted an appeal stating that truth is the first victim of war and calling for the Constitution to be observed and the SDF to be withdrawn from Iraq. This appeal has since been sent to Prime Minister Koizumi and other leading figures.

Yet Japan's peace Constitution is today on the endangered list. This Constitution with its ringing resolution that "never again shall we be visited with the horrors of war through the action of government," its proclamation that "sovereign power resides with the people," and its recognition that "all peoples of the world have the right to live in peace, free from fear and want" – this Constitution with Article 9's renunciation of war, its pledge not to maintain war potential, and its rejection of the right of belligerency – has been a source of hope and inspiration not only to war-ravaged Japan but to peace-loving peoples everywhere.

Despite this, we have seen a spate of unconstitutional policies adopted by the Koizumi administration since the turn of the century. To these, we have responded by calling upon all citizens to reread *Atarashii Kenpou no Hanashi* (The Story of the New Constitution, a middle-school reader on the new Constitution published by the Ministry of Education in August 1947) and to reassert their ideals. Confident that the Constitution of Japan is a model showing the way to a better future for all the world, we once more take up the ordinary citizens' cause and call on the government to live the Constitution.

Shimizu Hatoko
(President)

□■□ Forward-looking Discussion of the Constitution

Buraku Liberation League

ATTENTION IS currently focused on discussion of amending the Constitution, particularly Article 9. Sixty years since Japan lost the war, and 57 years since the Constitution was promulgated, the talk of amending the Constitution is moving forward on the assumption that the current Constitution no longer accords with current realities. Yet can we really say that this Constitution, with its ringing rejection of the use of force to settle international disputes, is behind the times?

As is clear from the Universal Declaration of Human Rights adopted by the Third Session of the United Nations General Assembly in 1948 when the scars of World War II were still fresh, war is the gravest affront to human rights, and it is the shared duty of all mankind to establish world peace and human rights. Moreover, these aims can only be achieved and maintained through ceaseless effort. The current Constitution, in sharp rebuke of and regret at Japan's having embarked upon the path of totalitarian militarism and a war of aggression, contains explicit renunciation of militarism and states as its core pillars popular sovereignty, pacifism, internationalism, and respect for human rights. This is all set out clearly in, for example, Article 11's respect for fundamental human rights, Article 13's respect for the people as individuals and guarantee of their right to life, liberty, and the pursuit of happiness, and Article 14's assertion of equality under the law.

Ever since the establishment of the predecessor National Levelers Association in 1922, and consistently since the war's end, the Buraku Liberation League has fought to give specific shape to these Constitutional precepts and to achieve their ends. And even though the BLL movement has achieved a measure of success, the state of Japanese society and government clearly still leaves much to be desired in terms of human rights and peace, including achieving the kind of peace that the Constitution envisions as a model for all humanity and ensuring respect for fundamental human rights. Especially noteworthy is the abject lack of legal redress for people who have been discriminated against or otherwise had their basic human rights violated. There is an urgent and imperative need to enact legislation prohibiting all forms of discrimination and providing for redress for victims of human rights violations.

Looking at the situation in Iraq, it is clear that Iraq is a war zone involving combat between the multilateral forces led by the U.S. and the U.K. and the resistance forces. As such, sending the Self-Defense Forces to Iraq under the guise of "humanitarian support," and especially taking part in multilateral force operations, is clearly in violation of the Constitution.

Any discussion of the Constitution has to be forward-looking with the people clearly instructing the government on the kind of state we want Japan to be while preserving the democratic principles – especially pacifism – embedded in the Constitution. And of course this also has to include profound contrition at the earlier war of aggression. Yet the current discussion has none of these essential features and is devoid of any such logic. Such discussion of amending the Constitution based entirely upon shallow assertions of national defense threaten to destroy Japanese pacifism and can only fan our neighbors' anxiety about a revival of Japan as a military power. With a Prime Minister such as Koizumi, who pushes through structural reforms abandoning society's disadvantaged to their plight and who makes repeated pilgrimages to Yasukuni Shrine, this is clearly no time to be moving to amend the Constitution.

Matsuoka Tooru
(Secretary General)

▢■▢ Restoring the Pride and Confidence
of the Meiji Constitution

Jinja Honchou (Association of Shinto Shrines)

THE CONSTITUTION IS the fundamental law setting forth the state's essential *reasons d'etre* based upon its history and social structure. Circumstances today vastly different from what they were when Japan regained its sovereignty half a century ago, it is incumbent upon us to completely rethink the current Constitution, adopted at the Occupation's behest and in the Occupation's mold, and to enact a new Constitution with a distinctly Japanese character grounded in our history and traditions.

Given this, Jinja Honchou maintains that, the Preamble aside, there is a pressing need to revise at least three main sections in the Constitution: Chapter I on the Emperor, Chapter II on the renunciation of war, and Chapter III on the rights and responsibilities of the people, especially the provisions relating to the separation of religion and state.

Looking first at Chapter I, the Imperial institution has been an integral part of Japan's religious and cultural traditions since time immemorial, and the Imperial dynasty is without peer or parallel, having been preserved intact for 125 generations down to the current Emperor. Recognizing the historic significance of the relationship between the Emperor and the people, we believe the Constitution should be amended to acknowledge the Emperor as the head of state and to reconsider his political and role authority. It is essential the wording be fully consistent with the Imperial institution's dignity.

Looking next at Article 9, there is an urgent national security need to revise this blanket renunciation of war. There are numerous situations today that Article 9's framework is inadequate to, including the need to act against international terrorism and the need for the Self-Defense Forces to play a greater international role. There is thus an urgent need to revise Arti especially its paragraph 2, so as to establish the SDF as a military force like any other nation's and to accord them all due honors and equal standing under international law.

Finally with regard to Article 20's secular separation of religion and state, the judicial and executive branches' continuing rejection of beautiful Japanese social customs and historical practices, the persistent interpretative flouting of the 1977 Supreme Court ruling allowing the city of Tsu to provide public funding for a grounds-purification ceremony by Shinto priests, and other inconsistencies have sown widespread confusion over the relationship between religion and the state, its institutions, local government bodies, and other public organizations. It is imperative that this situation, including rulings that visits by the Prime Minister and other public officials to Yasukuni Shrine are unconstitutional and findings that even reject the teaching of religious sensibilities in public schools, be rectified. In that sense, Article 20 should be revised by amending or deleting Paragraph 3 to provide institutional guarantees of freedom of religion.

In all of this, we feel it is necessary to draw up a new Constitution as soon as possible so as to regain the pride and confidence represented by the Meiji Constitution and the outstanding Constitutional monarchy it represented, to secure for Japan a position as an independent and sovereign state the equal of any other, and to allow the people to achieve spiritual independence as Japanese.

□■□ The Importance of Freedom of Religion and Separating Religion and State

Federation of New Religious Organizations of Japan

A RELATIVELY YOUNG religious body, the Federation of New Religious Organizations of Japan was founded in 1951. All of its member organizations – what have been called "new religions" – have joined together to defend freedom of religion, to promote religious education, and to contribute to world peace.

The FNROJ was established six years after the end of the war. This was also a time when many new religious organizations were being founded – so much so that it has been called "the rush hour of the gods." Yet such is not to say that the outpouring of new religious thought and the creation of numerous new religious organizations resulted from the postwar turmoil. Rather, this outpouring was because the Constitution guaranteed freedom of religion and all of these religions that had been shackled so long were finally free to find unfettered expression.

Because religious activity was sharply restricted before and during the war, it was impossible to found a new religion then even if you had a new revelation or a new interpretation of one of the sutras. The only options were to take up residence as a minor offshoot of one of the state-sanctioned religions or to practice your faith in secret under cover of a para-religious group. Yet even under these conditions, there were organizations that were ordered to disband for little reason.

Article 28 of the old Imperial Constitution of 1889 seemed to guarantee freedom of religion with its statement that "Japanese subjects shall, within limits not prejudicial to peace and order, and not antagonistic to their duties as subjects, enjoy freedom of religious belief." Yet this same Article also provided the rationale for oppression and soon became a tool of repression. With the end of the war, the state was no longer allowed to involve itself in religion, and the new Constitution boldly proclaimed freedom of religion in Article 20's "Freedom of religion is guaranteed to all" with none of the hedging of the old Meiji Constitution. The new Constitution also set forth the principle of separation of religion and the state and declared that "no religious organization shall receive any privileges from the State, nor exercise any political authority." This posited a rigorous separation between the state and any religion (religious organization), established the principle that the state could neither be involved in nor make use of any religion, and mandated that "the state and its organs shall refrain from religious education or any other religious activity."

Buoyed by this newfound freedom, the leaders of the new religious organizations agreed to not quarrel among themselves but to join hands in working to build a new Japan. Thus was the FNROJ born. As such, it may be said that the FNROJ was founded upon Article 20 of the new Constitution and cherishes this Article and its freedoms. Freedom of religion cannot be guaranteed in the absence of full freedom of thought and conscience, freedom of speech, press, and other forms of expression, and freedom of assembly and association. This is a fundamental tenet of basic human rights. From its very inception, the FNROJ has worked tirelessly and called for constant vigilance to ensure that this principle of separation of religion and state is not eroded and that freedom of religion is not threatened.

□■□ The Need to Understand and Observe the Constitution Better

Japan Buddhist Federation

THE PREAMBLE TO the Constitution speaks of our fervent desire for lasting peace free of the horrors of war; notes the need to banish tyranny and slavery, oppression and intolerance; and commits us to its lofty ideals in support of freedom.

With a membership of 58 denominations, 36 prefectural Buddhist associations, and 9 other Buddhist organizations, the Japan Buddhist Federation brings together the strengths of its 70,000-plus affiliated bodies. For over a century, the organization has been active in the Buddhist spirit of comforting others and living in peace and has worked to gain greater acceptance for Buddhist teachings and advance the cause of world peace.

Together with the Kyouhashinto Rengo, Japan Confederation of Christian Churches, Jinja Honchou, and Federation of New Religious Organizations of Japan, we are members of the Japan Religious League. In addition, we are the only Japanese Buddhist association representative member of the World Fellowship of Buddhists – an organization with members in over 140 countries – and have been actively cooperating not only with other Buddhist organizations but with other religious organizations across the spectrum.

Buddhism deplores the wanton taking of life and cherishes all living things. It is a teaching of respect for life in recognition of our myriad differences. Constantly on guard against the all-too-human tendency to get caught up in the self, Buddhism teaches reverence for the whole of life in its symbiotic complexity and stresses the importance of consideration for all of life and nature.

Backed by Buddhist teachings and Japan's peace Constitution, the JBF obviously seeks to eliminate war and achieve peace; but we also strive to, *inter alia*, promote the extension of human rights, preserve freedom of religion, ensure unbreached separation of religion and state, and promote the teaching of religious sentiment.

Cherishing Japan's peace Constitution born of the horrors of war, the Japanese people have made unstinting efforts for peace for over half a century, yet we are today at a new stage demanding we reaffirm the Constitution as the very keystone of our peace and prosperity. At the same time, given the way rampant materialism and mechanization have corroded the human spirit and exacerbated international conflict, it is essential we work to have the Constitution's lofty principles better understood and more faithfully observed if Japan and Japanese are to provide a global model.

Buddhist precepts

Faith in Buddhist teachings as they show the way to alleviating human anxiety and anguish caused by relations, contradictions, dependencies, and other worldly concerns is the path to freeing the pure spirit that resides in every person and achieving true self-consciousness.

Recognizing the profound web of cosmic inter-connections in which all depend upon, vie with, and exist in relation to each other, we seek to shed light on the path that modern civilization and mankind should take by acknowledging the dignity of each individual as an autonomous individual; respecting the chain of person-person, person-community, state-state, and other relationships in society; and articulating the ends and means of science and technology.

As well as developing the powers of observation and insight to enable us to see all things truly, making the utmost effort to banish wrong and endure humiliation, and move forward with our hearts as one, we seek to eradicate all violence and the threat of war, contribute to the betterment of mankind, and concentrate our minds on achieving lasting peace.

☐■☐ No-comments

A total of 25 high-profile organizations were asked to comment on the Constitution for this anthology. Thirteen provided opinion pieces, which appear in the previous pages of this section. Of the rest, some responded with notes explaining their reticence and some with not even that.

WE DO NOT REJECT the idea of discussing the Constitution. In fact, we have set up a working group specifically to survey what is being said and to organize it for later reference. This working group issued an interim report in July 2003, but that report was purely an effort to introduce the literature to date. There has been no specific debate on the issue since then, and we have not put a position together yet.

Japanese Trade Union Confederation

☐■☐

THE JAPAN TEACHERS UNION adopted the following policies at its 92nd extraordinary congress in March 2004.
1. Live the ideals in the Constitution and the Basic Law on Education and oppose moves to alter the Constitution for the worse.
1.1. While closely monitoring the activities of the research commissions, political parties, citizen groups, and the like, work to have our views expressed and reflected in a wide variety of channels to preserve the peace Constitution.
1.2. Establish a committee to respond to discussions of revising the Constitution and step up efforts in the Constitution's defense.

Japan Teachers Union

□ ■ □

THE JAPAN FEDERATION of Bar Associations has long been aware of the Constitution's importance, has established a Constitutional committee, and is currently collecting, analyzing, and verifying information on this. We are not, however, at a point where we can take a position on this.

Japan Federation of Bar Associations

□ ■ □

THE CONDITIONS GOVERNING the Institute's founding do not allow us to comment on the Constitution.

Japanese Institute of Certified Public Accountants

□ ■ □

WE ARE NOT in a position to comment on the Constitution.

Japan Patent Attorneys Association

□ ■ □

THE RED CROSS SOCIETY was founded to care for the war-wounded and sick irrespective of whether they are friends or foes. Since then, it has expanded its scope to also care for the victims of natural disasters, people suffering from AIDS and other illnesses, and others in need. Regardless of conditions in their home countries, all Red Cross Societies seek to provide equal treatment to everyone needing relief, and this means it is essential we do everything we can to ensure our activities can be readily understood and accepted by all. The Red Cross Society is thus constantly careful to maintain a position of neutrality and independence.

The minute the Red Cross Society takes a position favoring this or that state or this or that ideology or religion, that is the instant the Red Cross Society forfeits public trust in its neutrality. Should that trust be lost, the Red Cross Society's relief activities might be seen as politically motivated and it could prove impossible for us to do what needs to be done.

In Iraq, for example, even during the combat phase, the International Committee of the Red Cross supported medical care for citizens, worked to provide drinking water to all, conducted studies to find out what had happened to the missing, visited prisons, and more. These activities in Iraq would have been vastly more difficult had the International Committee tilted to favor the United States or Iraq. Neutrality is not just in a single time and place. Rather, it has to be a constant.

Given the need to maintain the Red Cross Society's neutrality, it would not be appropriate for the Japanese Red Cross Society to comment on the Constitution.

Japanese Red Cross Society

□■□

GIVEN THE SHRINE's public nature, we cannot judge the Constitution.

Yasukuni Shrine

□■□

THREE ORGANIZATIONS did not comment at all:
Nippon Keidanren (Japan Business Federation)
JA Zenchu (Central Union of Agricultural Co-operatives)
Japan Federation of Certified Public Tax Accountants' Associations

□■□

IN ADDITION, one welfare organization and one religious federation refused to allow their names to appear at all. Their wishes have been respected.

□□■ The Constitution of Japan

Promulgated on November 3, 1946
Came into effect on May 3, 1947

WE, THE JAPANESE PEOPLE, acting through our duly elected representatives in the National Diet, determined that we shall secure for ourselves and our posterity the fruits of peaceful cooperation with all nations and the blessings of liberty throughout this land, and resolved that never again shall we be visited with the horrors of war through the action of government, do proclaim that sovereign power resides with the people and do firmly establish this Constitution. Government is a sacred trust of the people, the authority for which is derived from the people, the powers of which are exercised by the representatives of the people, and the benefits of which are enjoyed by the people. This is a universal principle of mankind upon which this Constitution is founded. We reject and revoke all constitutions, laws, ordinances, and rescripts in conflict herewith.

We, the Japanese people, desire peace for all time and are deeply conscious of the high ideals controlling human relationship, and we have determined to preserve our security and existence, trusting in the justice and faith of the peace-loving peoples of the world. We desire to occupy an honored place in an international society striving for the preservation of peace, and the banishment of tyranny and slavery, oppression and intolerance for all time from the earth. We recognize that all peoples of the world have the right to live in peace, free from fear and want.

We believe that no nation is responsible to itself alone, but that laws of political morality are universal; and that obedience to such laws is incumbent upon all nations who would sustain their own sovereignty and justify their sovereign relationship with other nations.

We, the Japanese people, pledge our national honor to accomplish these high ideals and purposes with all our resources.

CHAPTER I
THE EMPEROR

ARTICLE 1. The Emperor shall be the symbol of the State and of the unity of the People, deriving his position from the will of the people with whom resides sovereign power.

ARTICLE 2. The Imperial Throne shall be dynastic and succeeded to in accordance with the Imperial House Law passed by the Diet.

ARTICLE 3. The advice and approval of the Cabinet shall be required for all acts of the Emperor in matters of state, and the Cabinet shall be responsible therefor.

ARTICLE 4. The Emperor shall perform only such acts in matters of state as are provided for in this Constitution and he shall not have powers related to government.

The Emperor may delegate the performance of his acts in matters of state as may be provided by law.

ARTICLE 5. When, in accordance with the Imperial House Law, a Regency is established, the Regent shall perform his acts in matters of state in the Emperor's name. In this case, paragraph one of the preceding article will be applicable.

ARTICLE 6. The Emperor shall appoint the Prime Minister as designated by the Diet.

The Emperor shall appoint the Chief Judge of the Supreme Court as designated by the Cabinet.

ARTICLE 7. The Emperor, with the advice and approval of the Cabinet, shall perform the following acts in matters of state on behalf of the people:

Promulgation of amendments of the constitution, laws, cabinet orders and treaties.

Convocation of the Diet.

Dissolution of the House of Representatives.

Proclamation of general election of members of the Diet.

Attestation of the appointment and dismissal of Ministers of State and other officials as provided for by law, and of full powers and credentials of Ambassadors and Ministers.

Attestation of general and special amnesty, commutation of punishment, reprieve, and restoration of rights.

Awarding of honors.

Attestation of instruments of ratification and other diplomatic documents as provided for by law.

Receiving foreign ambassadors and ministers.

Performance of ceremonial functions.

ARTICLE 8. No property can be given to, or received by, the Imperial House, nor can any gifts be made therefrom, without the authorization of the Diet.

CHAPTER II
RENUNCIATION OF WAR

ARTICLE 9. Aspiring sincerely to an international peace based on justice and order, the Japanese people forever renounce war as a sovereign right of the nation and the threat or use of force as means of settling international disputes.

In order to accomplish the aim of the preceding paragraph, land, sea, and air forces, as well as other war potential, will never be maintained. The right of belligerency of the state will not be recognized.

CHAPTER III
RIGHTS AND DUTIES OF THE PEOPLE

ARTICLE 10. The conditions necessary for being a Japanese national shall be determined by law.

ARTICLE 11. The people shall not be prevented from enjoying any of the fundamental human rights. These fundamental human rights guaranteed to the people by this Constitution shall be conferred upon the people of this and future generations as eternal and inviolate rights.

ARTICLE 12. The freedoms and rights guaranteed to the people by this Constitution shall be maintained by the constant endeavor of the people, who shall refrain from any abuse of these freedoms and rights and shall always be responsible for utilizing them for the public welfare.

ARTICLE 13. All of the people shall be respected as individuals. Their right to life, liberty, and the pursuit of happiness shall, to the extent that it does not interfere with the public welfare, be the supreme consideration in legislation and in other governmental affairs.

ARTICLE 14. All of the people are equal under the law and there shall be no discrimination in political, economic or social relations because of race, creed, sex, social status or family origin.

Peers and peerage shall not be recognized.

No privilege shall accompany any award of honor, decoration or any distinction, nor shall any such award be valid beyond the lifetime of the individual who now holds or hereafter may receive it.

ARTICLE 15. The people have the inalienable right to choose their public officials and to dismiss them.

All public officials are servants of the whole community and not of any group thereof.

Universal adult suffrage is guaranteed with regard to the election of public officials.

In all elections, secrecy of the ballot shall not be violated. A voter shall not be answerable, publicly or privately, for the choice he has made.

ARTICLE 16. Every person shall have the right of peaceful petition for the redress of damage, for the removal of public officials, for the enactment, repeal or amendment of laws, ordinances or regulations and for other matters; nor shall any person be in any way discriminated against for sponsoring such a petition.

ARTICLE 17. Every person may sue for redress as provided by law from the State or a public entity, in case he has suffered damage through illegal act of any public official.

ARTICLE 18. No person shall be held in bondage of any kind. Involuntary servitude, except as punishment for crime, is prohibited.

ARTICLE 19. Freedom of thought and conscience shall not be violated.

ARTICLE 20. Freedom of religion is guaranteed to all. No religious organization shall receive any privileges from the State, nor exercise any political authority.

No person shall be compelled to take part in any religious act, celebration, rite or practice.

The State and its organs shall refrain from religious education or any other religious activity.

ARTICLE 21. Freedom of assembly and association as well as speech, press and all other forms of expression are guaranteed.

No censorship shall be maintained, nor shall the secrecy of any means of communication be violated.

ARTICLE 22. Every person shall have freedom to choose and change his residence and to choose his occupation to the extent that it does not interfere with the public welfare.

Freedom of all persons to move to a foreign country and to divest themselves of their nationality shall be inviolate.

ARTICLE 23. Academic freedom is guaranteed.

ARTICLE 24. Marriage shall be based only on the mutual consent of both sexes and it shall be maintained through mutual cooperation with the equal rights of husband and wife as a basis.

With regard to choice of spouse, property rights, inheritance, choice of domicile, divorce and other matters pertaining to marriage and the family, laws shall be enacted from the standpoint of individual dignity and the essential equality of the sexes.

ARTICLE 25. All people shall have the right to maintain the minimum standards of wholesome and cultured living.

In all spheres of life, the State shall use its endeavors for the promotion and extension of social welfare and security, and of public health.

ARTICLE 26. All people shall have the right to receive an equal education correspondent to their ability, as provided by law.

All people shall be obligated to have all boys and girls under their protection receive ordinary education as provided for by law. Such compulsory education shall be free.

ARTICLE 27. All people shall have the right and the obligation to work.

Standards for wages, hours, rest and other working conditions shall be fixed by law.

Children shall not be exploited.

ARTICLE 28. The right of workers to organize and to bargain and act collectively is guaranteed.

ARTICLE 29. The right to own or to hold property is inviolable.

Property rights shall be defined by law, in conformity with the public welfare.

Private property may be taken for public use upon just compensation therefor.

ARTICLE 30. The people shall be liable to taxation as provided by law.

ARTICLE 31. No person shall be deprived of life or liberty, nor shall any other criminal penalty be imposed, except according to procedure established by law.

ARTICLE 32. No person shall be denied the right of access to the courts.

ARTICLE 33. No person shall be apprehended except upon warrant issued by a competent judicial officer which specifies the offense with which the person is charged, unless he is apprehended, the offense being committed.

ARTICLE 34. No person shall be arrested or detained without being at once informed of the charges against him or without the immediate privilege of counsel; nor shall he be detained without adequate cause; and upon demand of any person such cause must be immediately shown in open court in his presence and the presence of his counsel.

ARTICLE 35. The right of all persons to be secure in their homes, papers and effects against entries, searches and seizures shall not be impaired except upon warrant issued for adequate cause and particularly describing the place to be searched and things to be seized, or except as provided by Article 33.

Each search or seizure shall be made upon separate warrant issued by a competent judicial officer.

ARTICLE 36. The infliction of torture by any public officer and cruel punishments are absolutely forbidden.

ARTICLE 37. In all criminal cases the accused shall enjoy the right to a speedy and public trial by an impartial tribunal.

He shall be permitted full opportunity to examine all witnesses, and he shall have the right of compulsory process for obtaining witnesses on his behalf at public expense.

At all times the accused shall have the assistance of competent counsel who shall, if the accused is unable to secure the same by his own efforts, be assigned to his use by the State.

ARTICLE 38. No person shall be compelled to testify against himself.

Confession made under compulsion, torture or threat, or after prolonged arrest or detention shall not be admitted in evidence.

No person shall be convicted or punished in cases where the only proof against him is his own confession.

ARTICLE 39. No person shall be held criminally liable for an act which was lawful at the time it was committed, or of which he has been acquitted, nor shall he be placed in double jeopardy.

ARTICLE 40. Any person, in case he is acquitted after he has been arrested or detained, may sue the State for redress as provided by law.

CHAPTER IV
THE DIET

ARTICLE 41. The Diet shall be the highest organ of state power, and shall be the sole law-making organ of the State.

ARTICLE 42. The Diet shall consist of two Houses, namely the House of Representatives and the House of Councillors.

ARTICLE 43. Both Houses shall consist of elected members, representative of all the people.
The number of the members of each House shall be fixed by law.

ARTICLE 44. The qualifications of members of both Houses and their electors shall be fixed by law. However, there shall be no discrimination because of race, creed, sex, social status, family origin, education, property or income.

ARTICLE 45. The term of office of members of the House of Representatives shall be four years. However, the term shall be terminated before the full term is up in case the House of Representatives is dissolved.

ARTICLE 46. The term of office of members of the House of Councillors shall be six years, and election for half the members shall take place every three years.

ARTICLE 47. Electoral districts, method of voting and other matters pertaining to the method of election of members of both Houses shall be fixed by law.

ARTICLE 48. No person shall be permitted to be a member of both Houses simultaneously.

ARTICLE 49. Members of both Houses shall receive appropriate annual payment from the national treasury in accordance with law.

ARTICLE 50. Except in cases provided by law, members of both Houses shall be exempt from apprehension while the Diet is in session, and any members apprehended before the opening of the session shall be freed during the term of the session upon demand of the House.

ARTICLE 51. Members of both Houses shall not be held liable outside the House for speeches, debates or votes cast inside the House.

ARTICLE 52. An ordinary session of the Diet shall be convoked once per year.

ARTICLE 53. The Cabinet may determine to convoke extraordinary sessions of the Diet. When a quarter or more of the total members of either House makes the demand, the Cabinet must determine on such convocation.

ARTICLE 54. When the House of Representatives is dissolved, there must be a general election of members of the House of Representatives within forty (40) days from the date of dissolution, and the Diet must be convoked within thirty (30) days from the date of the election.

When the House of Representatives is dissolved, the House of Councillors is closed at the same time. However, the Cabinet may in time of national emergency convoke the House of Councillors in emergency session.

Measures taken at such session as mentioned in the proviso of the preceding paragraph shall be provisional and shall become null and void unless agreed to by the House of Representatives within a period of ten (10) days after the opening of the next session of the Diet.

ARTICLE 55. Each House shall judge disputes related to qualifications of its members. However, in order to deny a seat to any member, it is necessary to pass a resolution by a majority of two-thirds or more of the members present.

ARTICLE 56. Business cannot be transacted in either House unless one-third or more of total membership is present.

All matters shall be decided, in each House, by a majority of those present, except as elsewhere provided in the Constitution, and in case of a tie, the presiding officer shall decide the issue.

ARTICLE 57. Deliberation in each House shall be public. However, a secret meeting may be held where a majority of two-thirds or more of those members present passes a resolution therefor.

Each House shall keep a record of proceedings. This record

shall be published and given general circulation, excepting such parts of proceedings of secret session as may be deemed to require secrecy.

Upon demand of one-fifth or more of the members present, votes of the members on any matter shall be recorded in the minutes.

ARTICLE 58. Each House shall select its own president and other officials.

Each House shall establish its rules pertaining to meetings, proceedings and internal discipline, and may punish members for disorderly conduct. However, in order to expel a member, a majority of two-thirds or more of those members present must pass a resolution thereon.

ARTICLE 59. A bill becomes a law on passage by both Houses, except as otherwise provided by the Constitution.

A bill which is passed by the House of Representatives, and upon which the House of Councillors makes a decision different from that of the House of Representatives, becomes a law when passed a second time by the House of Representatives by a majority of two-thirds or more of the members present.

The provision of the preceding paragraph does not preclude the House of Representatives from calling for the meeting of a joint committee of both Houses, provided for by law.

Failure by the House of Councillors to take final action within sixty (60) days after receipt of a bill passed by the House of Representatives, time in recess excepted, may be determined by the House of Representatives to constitute a rejection of the said bill by the House of Councillors.

ARTICLE 60. The budget must first be submitted to the House of Representatives.

Upon consideration of the budget, when the House of Councillors makes a decision different from that of the House of Representatives, and when no agreement can be reached even through a joint committee of both Houses, provided for by law, or in the case of failure by the House of Councillors to take final action within thirty (30) days, the period of recess excluded, after the receipt of the budget passed by the House of Representatives, the decision of the House of Representatives shall be the decision of the Diet.

ARTICLE 61. The second paragraph of the preceding article applies also to the Diet approval required for the conclusion of treaties.

ARTICLE 62. Each House may conduct investigations in relation to government, and may demand the presence and testimony of witnesses, and the production of records.

ARTICLE 63. The Prime Minister and other Ministers of State may, at any time, appear in either House for the purpose of speaking on bills, regardless of whether they are members of the House or not. They must appear when their presence is required in order to give answers or explanations.

ARTICLE 64. The Diet shall set up an impeachment court from among the members of both Houses for the purpose of trying those judges against whom removal proceedings have been instituted.

Matters relating to impeachment shall be provided by law.

CHAPTER V
THE CABINET

ARTICLE 65. Executive power shall be vested in the Cabinet.

ARTICLE 66. The Cabinet shall consist of the Prime Minister, who shall be its head, and other Ministers of State, as provided for by law.

The Prime Minister and other Ministers of State must be civilians.

The Cabinet, in the exercise of executive power, shall be collectively responsible to the Diet.

ARTICLE 67. The Prime Minister shall be designated from among the members of the Diet by a resolution of the Diet. This designation shall precede all other business.

If the House of Representatives and the House of Councillors disagree and if no agreement can be reached even through a joint committee of both Houses, provided for by law, or the House of Councillors fails to make designation within ten (10) days, exclusive of the period of recess, after the House of Representatives has made designation, the decision of the House of Representatives shall be the decision of the Diet.

ARTICLE 68. The Prime Minister shall appoint the Ministers of State. However, a majority of their number must be chosen from among the members of the Diet.

The Prime Minister may remove the Ministers of State as he chooses.

ARTICLE 69. If the House of Representatives passes a non-confidence resolution, or rejects a confidence resolution, the Cabinet shall resign en masse, unless the House of Representatives is dissolved within ten (10) days.

ARTICLE 70. When there is a vacancy in the post of Prime Minister, or upon the first convocation of the Diet after a general election of members of the House of Representatives, the Cabinet shall resign en masse.

ARTICLE 71. In the cases mentioned in the two preceding articles, the Cabinet shall continue its functions until the time when a new Prime Minister is appointed.

ARTICLE 72. The Prime Minister, representing the Cabinet, submits bills, reports on general national affairs and foreign relations to the Diet and exercises control and supervision over various administrative branches.

ARTICLE 73. The Cabinet, in addition to other general administrative functions, shall perform the following functions:

Administer the law faithfully; conduct affairs of state.

Manage foreign affairs.

Conclude treaties. However, it shall obtain prior or, depending on circumstances, subsequent approval of the Diet.

Administer the civil service, in accordance with standards established by law.

Prepare the budget, and present it to the Diet.

Enact cabinet orders in order to execute the provisions of this Constitution and of the law. However, it cannot include penal provisions in such cabinet orders unless authorized by such law.

Decide on general amnesty, special amnesty, commutation of punishment, reprieve, and restoration of rights.

ARTICLE 74. All laws and cabinet orders shall be signed by the competent Minister of State and countersigned by the Prime Minister.

ARTICLE 75. The Ministers of State, during their tenure of office, shall not be subject to legal action without the consent of the Prime Minister. However, the right to take that action is not impaired hereby.

CHAPTER VI
JUDICIARY

ARTICLE 76. The whole judicial power is vested in a Supreme Court and in such inferior courts as are established by law.

No extraordinary tribunal shall be established, nor shall any organ or agency of the Executive be given final judicial power.

All judges shall be independent in the exercise of their conscience and shall be bound only by this Constitution and the laws.

ARTICLE 77. The Supreme Court is vested with the rule-making power under which it determines the rules of procedure and of practice, and of matters relating to attorneys, the internal discipline of the courts and the administration of judicial affairs.

Public procurators shall be subject to the rule-making power of the Supreme Court.

The Supreme Court may delegate the power to make rules for inferior courts to such courts.

ARTICLE 78. Judges shall not be removed except by public impeachment unless judicially declared mentally or physically incompetent to perform official duties. No disciplinary action against judges shall be administered by any executive organ or agency.

ARTICLE 79. The Supreme Court shall consist of a Chief Judge and such number of judges as may be determined by law; all such judges excepting the Chief Judge shall be appointed by the Cabinet.

The appointment of the judges of the Supreme Court shall be reviewed by the people at the first general election of members of the House of Representatives following their appointment, and shall be reviewed again at the first general election of members of the House of Representatives after a lapse of ten (10) years, and in the same manner thereafter.

In cases mentioned in the foregoing paragraph, when the majority of the voters favors the dismissal of a judge, he shall be dismissed.

Matters pertaining to review shall be prescribed by law.

The judges of the Supreme Court shall be retired upon the attainment of the age as fixed by law.

All such judges shall receive, at regular stated intervals, adequate compensation which shall not be decreased during their terms of office.

ARTICLE 80. The judges of the inferior courts shall be appointed by the Cabinet from a list of persons nominated by the Supreme Court. All such judges shall hold office for a term of ten (10) years with privilege of reappointment, provided that they shall be retired upon the attainment of the age as fixed by law.

The judges of the inferior courts shall receive, at regular stated intervals, adequate compensation which shall not be decreased during their terms of office.

ARTICLE 81. The Supreme Court is the court of last resort with power to determine the constitutionality of any law, order, regulation or official act.

ARTICLE 82. Trials shall be conducted and judgment declared publicly.

Where a court unanimously determines publicity to be dangerous to public order or morals, a trial may be conducted privately, but trials of political offenses, offenses involving the press or cases wherein the rights of people as guaranteed in Chapter III of this Constitution are in question shall always be conducted publicly.

CHAPTER VII
FINANCE

ARTICLE 83. The power to administer national finances shall be exercised as the Diet shall determine.

ARTICLE 84. No new taxes shall be imposed or existing ones modified except by law or under such conditions as law may prescribe.

ARTICLE 85. No money shall be expended, nor shall the State obligate itself, except as authorized by the Diet.

ARTICLE 86. The Cabinet shall prepare and submit to the Diet for its consideration and decision a budget for each fiscal year.

ARTICLE 87. In order to provide for unforeseen deficiencies in the budget, a reserve fund may be authorized by the Diet to be expended upon the responsibility of the Cabinet.

The Cabinet must get subsequent approval of the Diet for all payments from the reserve fund.

ARTICLE 88. All property of the Imperial Household shall belong to the State. All expenses of the Imperial Household shall be appropriated by the Diet in the budget.

ARTICLE 89. No public money or other property shall be expended or appropriated for the use, benefit or maintenance of any religious institution or association, or for any charitable, educational or benevolent enterprises not under the control of public authority.

ARTICLE 90. Final accounts of the expenditures and revenues of the State shall be audited annually by a Board of Audit and submitted by the Cabinet to the Diet, together with the statement of audit, during the fiscal year immediately following the period covered.

The organization and competency of the Board of Audit shall be determined by law.

ARTICLE 91. At regular intervals and at least annually the Cabinet shall report to the Diet and the people on the state of national finances.

CHAPTER VIII
LOCAL SELF-GOVERNMENT

ARTICLE 92. Regulations concerning organization and operations of local public entities shall be fixed by law in accordance with the principle of local autonomy.

ARTICLE 93. The local public entities shall establish assemblies as their deliberative organs, in accordance with law.

The chief executive officers of all local public entities, the members of their assemblies, and such other local officials as may be determined by law shall be elected by direct popular vote within their several communities.

ARTICLE 94. Local public entities shall have the right to manage their property, affairs and administration and to enact their own regulations within law.

ARTICLE 95. A special law, applicable only to one local public entity, cannot be enacted by the Diet without the consent of the majority of the voters of the local public entity concerned, obtained in accordance with law.

CHAPTER IX
AMENDMENTS

ARTICLE 96. Amendments to this Constitution shall be initiated by the Diet, through a concurring vote of two-thirds or more of all the members of each House and shall thereupon be submitted to the people for ratification, which shall require the affirmative vote of a majority of all votes cast thereon, at a special referendum or at such election as the Diet shall specify.

Amendments when so ratified shall immediately be promulgated by the Emperor in the name of the people, as an integral part of this Constitution.

CHAPTER X
SUPREME LAW

ARTICLE 97. The fundamental human rights by this Constitution guaranteed to the people of Japan are fruits of the age-old struggle of man to be free; they have survived the many exacting tests for durability and are conferred upon this and future generations in trust, to be held for all time inviolate.

ARTICLE 98. This Constitution shall be the supreme law of the nation and no law, ordinance, imperial rescript or other act of government, or part thereof, contrary to the provisions hereof, shall have legal force or validity.

The treaties concluded by Japan and established laws of nations shall be faithfully observed.

ARTICLE 99. The Emperor or the Regent as well as Ministers of State, members of the Diet, judges, and all other public officials have the obligation to respect and uphold this Constitution.

CHAPTER XI
SUPPLEMENTARY PROVISIONS

ARTICLE 100. This Constitution shall be enforced as from the day when the period of six months will have elapsed counting from the day of its promulgation.

The enactment of laws necessary for the enforcement of this Constitution, the election of members of the House of Councillors and the procedure for the convocation of the Diet and other preparatory procedures necessary for the enforcement of this Constitution may be executed before the day prescribed in the preceding paragraph.

ARTICLE 101. If the House of Councillors is not constituted before the effective date of this Constitution, the House of Representatives shall function as the Diet until such time as the House of Councillors shall be constituted.

ARTICLE 102. The term of office for half the members of the House of Councillors serving in the first term under this Constitution shall be three years. Members falling under this category shall be determined in accordance with law.

ARTICLE 103. The Ministers of State, members of the House of Representatives and judges in office on the effective date of this Constitution, and all other public officials who occupy positions corresponding to such positions as are recognized by this Constitution shall not forfeit their positions automatically on account of the enforcement of this Constitution unless otherwise specified by law. When, however, successors are elected or appointed under the provisions of this Constitution, they shall forfeit their positions as a matter of course.

Index

Made in the USA
Lexington, KY
05 December 2010